THE
WAY OF
NO WAY

THE
WAY OF
NO WAY

Solving
the Jeet
Kune Do
Riddle

Jerry Beasley, Ed.D.

PALADIN PRESS
BOULDER, COLORADO

Also by Jerry Beasley:

In Search of the Ultimate Martial Art:
  The Jeet Kune Do Experience

The Way of No Way:
Solving the Jeet Kune Do Riddle
by Jerry Beasley

Copyright © 1992 by Jerry Beasley

ISBN 0-87364-668-1
Printed in the United States of America

Published by Paladin Press, a division of
Paladin Enterprises, Inc., P.O. Box 1307,
Boulder, Colorado 80306, USA.
(303) 443-7250

Direct inquires and/or orders to the above address.

Contents

To Cody

Acknowledgments

Let me first thank my wife Gina who, as a professional editor, took the rough copy and developed it into a manuscript.

The photographers who assisted me include Jack Jeffers and Ric Anderton.

My thanks to sparring partners Bo Howell, Jim Quesenberry, and Chip Reeves. Thanks also to Cliff Lenderman, who is destined to become a martial arts movie star. I also wish to thank Jim Coleman (*Black Belt*), John Soet (*Inside Karate*), and Dave Cater (*Inside Kung-Fu*) for publishing my articles about jeet kune do. Regarding my own knowledge of JKD, I have primarily Dan Inosanto and Joe Lewis to thank. To the late Bruce Lee, whose writings and films I have studied often, I express my respect.

Finally, I wish to acknowledge Jon Ford and those at Paladin Press who have helped make my books possible.

Introduction

This book may well represent the first objective study and analysis of the art and practice of jeet kune do. JKD can be defined. JKD can be coordinated, taught, experienced, and, above all, understood. No body of information or physical practice is above comprehension. JKD has been shadowed in myth and misinformation—perhaps to hide its owners' limitations, or perhaps because it was in a continual state of flux. Bruce Lee did not complete his art of JKD. When he died, he left his students with memories and pieces of a puzzle.

Rather than sort the pieces and solve the puzzle, Lee's followers seemed to thrive on the promotion of misinformation. Because an art has no boundaries, it does not follow that its performers have none. We can study an art both through its performers and any written, photographed, or otherwise recorded events that detail its existence.

This study reflects my twenty-year interest in the practice of the art of JKD. Utilizing scientific methods, I have sought to record and analyze available information. I feel satisfied that the information contained in this book will be of value to JKD practitioners. The pursuit of knowledge and true learning begin when we ask, "Why?" I have asked this question about JKD. I hope the results of my endless investigation will be of use to others. I have in no way attempted to belittle JKD practitioners; rather, I have sought to understand them and to help them better understand their own art.

There are, no doubt, those who will consider my efforts of no consequence. We refer to such closed mindedness (associated with the so-called JKD elite, in this case) as ethnocentrism—the belief that the views of one's group are somehow more important or superior to those of another. I have sought to maintain objectivity by refusing to join any JKD group, society, clan, association, or organization. Lee was vehemently opposed to group control for the simple reason that it tends to limit individuals to the beliefs, practices, and values held by those who lead the group.

Today, JKD is divided into two factions, each claiming to teach the true way. I have witnessed in no other martial art the type of elitism, ethnocentrism, and closed mindedness that prospers in JKD. At the same time, no other art offers the potential for freedom of expression that JKD does. If our goal is simply to learn, then JKD is an exceptional opportunity. The door to discovery is open. If our goal is simply to identify with Lee, that, too, can be achieved, but at a considerable cost, for it is those who cling so passionately to the name who sacrifice their own identities and create the political havoc that could annihilate JKD.

In the end, the journey, the experience, the knowledge of JKD is to be desired at each level and in each group. I hope that this book will hasten your pursuit of JKD.

CHAPTER 1
Developing a Science for JKD

I believe that JKD is a most important theory. When properly applied, it can improve the performance of any art or any practitioner. I consider JKD the most significant contribution of the twentieth century to martial arts theory. I studied under Dan Inosanto in twelve (camp/seminar) installments between 1984 and 1988 and logged hundreds of hours researching, practicing, and discovering with JKD apprentice and associate instructors. In addition, I practiced the fighting concepts of Bruce Lee with Joe Lewis through most of the 1980s.

But I feel certain that it was my perseverance in college that allowed me to develop a definition for JKD. I spent most of the '70s in college earning bachelor's, master's, and doctoral degrees. In addition to practicing martial arts, I learned and applied scientific methods of research (required at both the master's and doctoral levels).

I needed only apply my education to combining Dan's theoretical knowledge with the practical experience proved by Joe—a kind of yin/yang approach—in order to redact the concepts of JKD and put the puzzle together.

In recent months, I have promoted the "original art" view of JKD. Limited as it is (to the performer's attributes), it represents an initial phase of JKD. Lee was obviously less than satisfied with what he had done and abandoned the "original art" in favor of the concepts method.

In the interview with Inosanto which follows, I think Dan makes a most important observation: you must be able to trace your line to have JKD. And one must be able to present a clear understanding of the concepts to call it JKD. At some point, Lee supposedly said something to the effect of, "JKD is like a boat. Once it has been used to get you across the river, it should be discarded." But when your boat is worth a lot of money, it's kind of difficult to part with it.

Lewis discarded it. Inosanto teaches kali and silat. Yet one can recognize JKD in his movements, his styles, his personality. It is safe to say that those who cling to the name lack a sense of ownership. As Dan might say, if they do "this" and say "this," they can call it "this." But in the final analysis, to say "this" and do "this" is of importance. To call it JKD is to betray a trust. JKD is an experience, not something to be sold, borrowed, or bought. Associations, memberships—even family relations—are but false illusions for the person who needs a name or a title.

In the summer of 1988, I completed my book, *In Search of the Ultimate Martial Art: The Jeet Kune Do Experience*, for Paladin Press. I presented the final chapter of the original manuscript to Inosanto for review. On our way to the Great Smoky Mountain JKD Camp (we had been shooting photos at a lake near Brasstown, NC), I asked him for his opinion of my research and recorded his comments.

Beasley: Dan, my thesis breaks JKD down into three areas. In the first part, JKD would be a theory engaging six principles that compose conceptual JKD. The second part is physical—the skills being practiced. At this time, when people see JKD they identify Thai boxing and kali. When Bruce Lee was at the helm, they expected to see wing chun and kickboxing.

Inosanto: They expected to see wing chun, but it's a blend. Like he [Lee] told me, it may not fit you. And he's right. I had to adopt certain things that I like. For example, where is an area that most people are not necessarily educated? Weapons! One thing Malaysian arts and Indonesian arts do—even though you may already be good empty-hand to empty-hand—they put in that twelve-inch implement, the knife, and it changes the technology completely.

See, I wouldn't throw a spinning side kick. I wouldn't throw a straight side kick. Well, maybe about knee level. The roundhouse I would watch very closely because it could be too dangerous [to use]. You have to go very, very low with that kick. The technology can change. In some cases, even a jab might be out. That's why I put a lot of kali into the system [JKD]. Because it was workable. I looked at the concepts laid down by Bruce. He told me that there were really few systems that practice, for example, a sophisticated five ways of attack. With weaponry and empty hands? Yes. Do they have attack by combination with the weapon and with empty hands? Yes, they do. Do they have progressive indirect attack? Yes, they do. Do they practice HIA, hand immobilization attack? Yes. Do they have attack by drawing? Yes, they do. Then it fits the criteria. Therefore, I can add it. It may not be the same thing Bruce used. But they use the focus glove. Do they use a form of boxing? Yes, they do. Do they have a form of kicking? Yes.

Beasley: So the concepts dictate the skill to be used?

Inosanto: Right. So if you can add it, then it's valuable.

Beasley: Again, in my thesis on JKD, we see the theoretical (the concepts or principles); the physical, which at this time is identified through kali, Thai, silat, etc.; and an essential component, the family or social part of JKD.

Inosanto: Right. And ...

Beasley: In order for JKD to be fully examined or defined, one actually needs to review all three components (theoretical, physical, social). At the same time, one could potentially concentrate only on the theoretical level and apply it to any art. This could actually be done outside of the family or the physical skills (Thai, kali, silat) currently being taught.

Inosanto: That is perfect! You hit it right on the button. That's bingo right there.

Beasley: That being the case, JKD can actually be defined.

Therefore, in discussing JKD, you could, in effect, ask a person to show you his interpretation of a specific principle to discover his understanding and application of JKD.

Inosanto: It can.

Beasley: You could then immediately recognize whether or not it is JKD.

Inosanto: But, now the family is a different thing. As much as I, let's say, admire Elvis Presley, I can't be Elvis Presley [or in his family]. If you said, all right, give the fifty songs that Elvis made famous, and I sang them, can I say that I am in the Presley family? I might even sound like him. But I can't be in the family because I have to be related. It has to come through a line. Let's say I was a fairly good singer. I sang his songs pretty good. An imitation of Elvis, right? Still I am not Elvis Presley. I am not in his family. Now that's what people do. They go, well if I can do "this" and "this," then I must be "this" [doing JKD]. But you can't. Because that must come through a family line. That's all I am saying.

Beasley: That is an excellent point. As you say, one must have all three elements—knowledge of the theory [concepts or principles], skill in the physical performance, and the ability to trace his principal instructor directly to Bruce Lee.

Inosanto: Right! That's all it is. See, now a guy could be very, very good. Have the first two. But there must be the family line. That's all there is to it. There is the Jun Fan gung fu system, and that's the base system which Bruce handed down to us. It can be expanded. It can be taken away. Some people are dogmatic. There is a group that says JKD is "this" because these are the original techniques handed to me by Bruce Lee. And this was when he was teaching JKD. He didn't call it a concept at that time. But he always mentioned that it was a concept. But those guys didn't want to hear it. Because you have to have a name. If a guy says, what do you practice? You say, eclectic system. They go, what is that? You guys don't even have a name. See, you've got to call it something. If you see a guy walking down the street, what do you call him? Man? Boy? You have to give him a name. Bruce was sorry he coined the term jeet kune do—the way of the intercepting fist. Jerry, you . . . uh . . . that's the best article. I am not just telling you this. Right now I am speaking from my heart. That's the best article I've ever read on JKD from a person outside the clan. No one has ever seen that. But you can write it in so many articles, say it in so many ways, and it's still going to be misinterpreted. That's the nature of the animal, Jerry.

• • • • •

Inosanto's critique of my research provided me with both the confidence and the incentive to continue my efforts. I had long since lost any desire to become a "JKD instructor." I was not ready to develop still another path as a JKD researcher. At one point I wanted to please the JKD seniors. But the information that I was to uncover was so personally rewarding and challenging that I quickly lost contact with any political system. Ahead of me lay the quest for pure knowledge.

THE SYSTEM OF EXPLORATION

Michael DePasquale Jr., publisher of *Karate International* magazine, encouraged me to write a JKD column for him in 1989, after he read my first book. Here was an opportunity to make my research available on a monthly basis. I was overwhelmed with the response to my views. Not only did some of the JKD elite offer encouragement, but readers from around the world were kind enough to offer criticism, praise, and information. In this book, I want to share the processing of the JKD information that I have obtained. Just as important, the reader should understand that all of the theories, concepts, and opinions have already been expressed openly and received by the public with overall positive acceptance.

Here, chronicled for the first time, are important articles that provide a step-by-step analysis of the development of redactive JKD methodology. The first step was to identify a scientific base for the understanding of JKD. This was accomplished in the April and June 1990 issues of *Karate International* in the articles entitled "An Introduction to Junfanology" and "How to Study Jeet Kune Do."

▼

AN INTRODUCTION TO JUNFANOLOGY

At some point in my effort to study jeet kune do, I realized that the circumstances of the art's emergence were infinitely more interesting than the art itself. In the last few years, I have attempted to develop a method for studying "about" JKD. Note the difference: When one studies JKD, one is involved in attempting to understand the physical and philosophical concepts presented by those who are said to be knowledgeable in the field. However, to study about JKD affords one the opportunity to both learn the physical and philosophical concepts and to recognize the interplay of vital forces which control the dissemination of knowledge about JKD. In other words, it is necessary to step outside of the subject in order to establish a value-free understanding of the practice of JKD.

This method of studying (about) JKD will henceforth be termed "junfanology." Of course, Jun Fan was Bruce Lee's Chinese name, so it is fitting and proper that we identify this study as such. More importantly, however, we have added the "ology" as recognition of the scientific procedures involved in the intended study. Thus, junfanology is the science of studying about JKD.

The word "science" makes reference to a systematic and rigorous method of gathering and organizing information. This method involves identifying problems, formulating hypotheses, collecting data, testing hypotheses, and verifying results. Junfanology, unlike JKD, should be less concerned with the development and use of parables and vague analogies, and primarily concerned with functional information derived from the scientific method. While the term JKD is used to denote the physical/philosophical concepts espoused by Lee and his followers, junfanology finds interest in political, economic, and historical facts which may be said to influence the current application of the JKD system.

Junfanology as the science of studying about JKD is, in fact, already far more popular than the actual performing and practicing of the physical/philosophical concepts of JKD. Obviously, there are considerably more individuals who read about and talk about JKD than who physically practice it. Although Lee passed away more than fifteen years ago, only a handful of individuals have been identified as "givers of the truth," those who can teach JKD. Thus, JKD has been kept alive by junfanologists—individuals engaged in the practice of studying about JKD.

We must immediately distinguish between the amateur and the professional junfanologist. Generally, we think of the word "profession" as referring to anyone who receives money for his efforts. This popular definition of "professional" has been accepted as a result of the professional-versus-amateur (paid-versus-nonpaid) status used in sports. A profession in the strict sense maintains a recognizable and definable body of knowledge. Members of a profession have completed a standard method of study and recognize an internal method of governance. More importantly, there presently exists much argument concerning what is now being billed as "real" or "original" JKD versus the concepts method that is widely practiced.

The JKD that I remember from the early 1970s was, as Lee taught and promoted it, a style—the style of scientific street fighting. When I participated in the new JKD of the '80s—the concepts method—I had difficulty understanding the seemingly endless variations of arts and systems required to tap into the flow (that point of being one with your opponent). During the flow, no style exists. One simply answers an attack with an attack. The highest level—the JKD level—is to intercept the attack, to be so attuned to the opponent's energy, both physical and mental, that you recognize and intercept it before he can complete it.

There are two distinct ways of reaching this ultimate level of ability (JKD). The concepts method teaches a variety of arts to be used at appropriate ranges. When mastered, JKD is the ability to blend with any form of attack. A second method, the original JKD, presents the empty-hand fencing approach wherein a series of trapping, striking, and grappling skills are honed to perfection. Thus, any attack can be met with immediate response.

To further illustrate the variations of the two methods, let's examine diving as a physical skill. One school of thought might be to teach different ways of diving so that the practitioner is prepared to dive from a high drop-off area (a cliff, for example), in shallow water, and in salt water. The list goes on. Surely, the diver who learns the various concepts associated with the practice is prepared for all methods of entry.

Ultimately, one must enter the water. Lee apparently sought to understand the commonality among all forms of entry, whether high and looping or shallow and sleek. What components result in success? What attributes exist that lead to success in the entry? Although Lee did not write this, sports researchers have concluded that success in any competition (from streetfighting to bingo) rests on attributes, strategy, and chance.

We can train for attributes and strategy, but we can prepare merely to the best of our ability for chance (luck). Lee's original art encompassed a strategy for developing specific attributes necessary in combat. His intercepting fist method (strategy) was functional only for the one who possessed the appropriate attributes, e.g., speed, power, sensitivity, accuracy, instinct, and so on. Thus, to utilize original JKD, wherein the strategy was to intercept, one must develop the attributes. However, to develop conceptual JKD, one would likely spend less time developing attributes and more time working on strategy. In this case, the strategy is to develop expertise at various ranges, utilizing numerous arts under an array of conditions.

Imagine, for example, that you are a tae kwon do stylist. You have developed the fastest, strongest, and most accurate side kick. Your strategy is to intercept any attack with this kick. For the best effect, the kick must be fully extended. In most cases, you can't be beaten. However, one attribute lacking in your kick is effectiveness at close range (toe to toe). When your back is against a wall, a person standing next to you cannot be intercepted. Additionally, you, like most others, could be blindsided (hit from behind without seeing the attack coming—chance).

By utilizing the concepts method, you would, of course, incorporate close-range fighting skills to eliminate any disadvantage. The strategy for conceptual JKD is advanced and, in effect, far superior to that of most arts, especially those emphasizing a particular range or skill, e.g., the shotokan reverse punch. However, one can be knowledgeable in just so many arts and ranges and be lacking in attributes (power, speed, sensitivity, etc.). Such a person might be defeated easily.

Historically, the most successful fighters have developed only a few techniques to perfection. Bill Wallace used only three kicks and was undefeated in kickboxing. Joe Lewis concentrated only on the side kick and forefist strike to win countless fights. Even Bruce Lee's intercepting fist was developed to a level of perfection that assured victory.

Lee's "style" of JKD, I am convinced, was not originally the concepts method. Lee had a system of intercepting. He had specific skills, angles, and methods of utilization. What made JKD work for him was command of his attributes. Lee was simply the strongest, fastest person he could possibly be. His JKD, when performed by someone else, is very much dependent upon the attributes of the performer. As one's attributes are diminished due to age, lack of practice, injury, and so on, the ability to perform original JKD is slighted as well.

Few people understand the differences between the two methods. Through my columns in *Karate International*, I have promoted the idea of original JKD as well as conceptual JKD.

The goal is not to pick sides or gain support. As scientists, as junfanologists, we seek only objective knowledge of events and circumstances.

Historical junfanology concerns itself with documenting the life and times of Lee and includes the development of the system called JKD. Numerous articles and books make a plethora of information available to the junfanologist. Amateur junfanologists interested in historical data generally collect every written word concerning Lee and organize these articles in various ways. While mere collection is of use, it is the scientific analysis and treatment of acquired data that serve as a basis for junfanology.

As you can see, the practice of junfanology already exists. We have simply sought to provide a name for the practice and to organize the parameters of the study.

HOW TO STUDY JEET KUNE DO

As a science, junfanology follows a standard method of identifying problems, formulating hypotheses, collecting data, testing hypotheses, and formulating and verifying results. Junfanology may be pursued in four areas of interest: historical, behavioral, physical, and philosophical.

Junfanology is an organized method of learning about Bruce Lee (historical), his art (physical), his philosophy (philosophical), and his associates (behavioral). The majority of junfanologists (people who study Lee) are primarily interested in historical junfanology. There has been far more written about the life and times of Lee than about his art of JKD.

An area that is gaining in popularity is that of behavioral junfanology. On more than a few occasions, I have spent hours on the phone with fellow junfanologists who have collected data concerning political, sociological, psychological, and economic ramifications of the science. Of particular interest to most is the political structure of the JKD society and the JKD family.

Junfanology may be a new word to most of us, but it adequately describes a process of learning information that has been utilized since the mid-1960s. As more and more individuals join in the science of junfanology, leaders in the various branches of study will undoubtedly surface. There is, in fact, a discernable difference between being a Lee fan and being a junfanologist. While the fan simply reads articles and engages in conversations, the junfanologist collects data (facts or information collected for the purpose of analysis) and forms hypotheses.

While the typical Lee fan is just scanning the latest gossip columns or reading the latest articles, the junfanologist is taking notes, recording issue dates and volume numbers, noting authorship, and seeking documentation for any facts that are unveiled. The junfanologist, to verify facts, sorts articles and cross-checks for duplicated publication of information. While fans may base their opinions on gossip, or hearsay and what they think they remember, junfanologists base their opinions on documented evidence.

As a junfanologist, I had a most difficult time analyzing data about physical junfanology (JKD) from published materials (books and magazines geared toward fans). After hearing known JKD instructors talk about their understanding of JKD, I still found the analysis of data to be frustrating. It was only after hearing the concepts firsthand that I was able to form reasonable hypotheses and eventually organize my thoughts into the principles of JKD. From those principles I was eventually able to develop the JKD matrix.

JEET KUNE DO IN THE 1970S AND 1980S

In the 1970s, JKD was virtually nonexistent. Except for an occasional article about Bruce Lee, little information regarding the actual practice of JKD was available. Lee had certified no instructors in his art. Joe Lewis, the top JKD kickboxer, adopted more orthodox boxing methods and introduced full-contact karate without emphasizing JKD. Dan Inosanto, Lee's appointed spokesperson, had developed the Kali Academy and continued teaching JKD simply as one course of the curriculum offered. Lee had been adamant about not letting his students teach others what they had learned about JKD. And, being true to their sifu, the known students of JKD were very selective about who could and could not enter the tight-knit JKD group.

By the late 1980s, the desire for JKD identification had resulted in the proliferation of unauthorized JKD schools throughout the country. Since most people had heard of Lee's JKD (hardly anyone knew how to identify it), the bogus JKD instructors enjoyed unchallenged authority to teach whatever they could and call it JKD. Responding in part to widespread misinformation, Inosanto began teaching seminars to those interested in learning more about JKD.

Inosanto taught the concepts of JKD through the Filipino art of kali. The seminar incorporated some of the original JKD training methods, trapping skills, and focus glove routines, but the bulk of the subject matter concerned kali.

Kali, a sophisticated martial art, could be used to demonstrate any of the principles of JKD. Sensitivity, range, strategy, and other concepts were easily demonstrated through kali. Through his teaching, Inosanto was not only able to promote the Filipino martial art; to some extent, he was able to hold to an agreement not to teach that which Lee had specifically asked him not to.

The public readily accepted the kali version of JKD. As seminar attendees requested new information, Inosanto introduced Thai boxing, savate, and eventually Indonesian silat. To the vast majority of JKD enthusiasts, JKD meant practicing a combination of kali, Thai boxing, wing chun, and silat. Because this sampling of arts did not resemble what Lee had performed in several films and books, an explanation was provided: what we had seen Lee perform on camera was referred to as theatrical JKD. Lee only did this for effect; it was not really JKD.

JKD writers during the early and mid-1980s added to the confusion by identifying with various Lee riddles, e.g., "using no way as way and no art as art." Additionally, a popular JKD video performer enhanced the JKD mentality by making it apparent that he really was unsure of whether his defense would be kali, savate, wing chun, etc. Throughout the series, the spokesperson implied that JKD consisted of various arts which could not be distinguished easily at any given time. One simply had to respond with a kali trap, savate kick, or Thai elbow, not knowing from one minute to the next what would take place.

To the novice martial artist, JKD required knowledge of several dozen martial arts and the ability to use each art at the appropriate times. Lee's emphasis on chiseling away the nonessentials was quickly being replaced with the addition of as much as possible in hopes that one would know the right counter for the corresponding attack. Because JKD supposedly had no boundaries, the 1980s performers attempted to demonstrate that they, too, were limitless. As long as Inosanto had approved the art (and Lee had, to some degree, researched it), it must be JKD. At some point, it became important to identify all the arts (a "yuppie" mentality) in order to give a convincing JKD performance.

If it can be said that we began the decade of the '80s with little knowledge of JKD, then by the late '80s we had learned little more than we knew when we began. Sure, we had been taught this art and that one, but what about a definition for JKD? *Inside Kung-Fu* Editor Dave Cater voiced his readers' growing concerns by penning the controversial editorial, "Using No Sense as Sense," for the August 1988 issue. His poignant question, "What the hell is JKD?" was one I had asked often of JKD instructors.

ANSWERING THE JKD DILEMMA

In the January 1989 issue of *Inside Kung-Fu*, Cater allowed me the opportunity to test my new definition of JKD.

▼

Since the original editorial "Using No Sense as Sense" appeared in the August 1988 issue, Inside Kung-Fu *has received more than thirty letters and twice as many phone calls commenting on the pros and cons of the magazine's stance. Many of those letters have appeared in print. This letter, written by Dr. Jerry Beasley, a career martial artist and professor at Radford (Va.) University, is the first to offer a detailed explanation of the jeet kune do system.*

—*Dave* Cater

In response to your timely August editorial, "Using No Sense as Sense," which asks the question, "What the hell is JKD?," let me simply add that many share your frustrations. At 32, Bruce Lee may well have had in his mind a framework for jeet kune do, but he failed to put it down on paper.

However, careful observation and testing may result in an organized definition of JKD.

In 1983, I attended the first of a dozen or more JKD seminars with the intent of writing a book about JKD. I found that, while thousands of pages had been published about JKD, the experience I gathered from the seminar was very different than the information I had recorded through articles. What had been previously written about JKD did little for me in the way of assisting with my understanding of the concept. Definitions such as JKD is the "style of no style" and "the way of no way" mean very little to the uninitiated. Moreover, these definitions and my favorite, "either you know it or you don't, and that's that!" are the source of major frustration. It may be argued that these definitions have become JKD's own "classical mess."

Since I am not an instructor of JKD, I was not influenced politically by the JKD Society. College professors are required to

Figure 1

In this sequence from the mid-1970s, Beasley demonstrates JKD concepts that had been applied to karate competition via Joe Lewis. As opponents square off (Figure 1), Beasley utilizes attack by drawing or ABD (Figure 2) and immobilization attack by incorporating a knee/elbow destruction (Figure 3).

Figure 2

Figure 3

In Figure 4, he follows with a forward side (closest weapon to nearest target), a straight punch (Figure 5), and an inside kick (Figure 6).

Figure 4

Figure 5

Figure 6

research and publish as a means of attaining tenure and promotions. Here, then, was my motive. In 1983, I began an ethnographic analysis of JKD. My methodology included observation techniques, personal experience, interviews, and other qualitative data acquisition procedures. The data from the five-year study then was examined through content analysis to form the resultant observations. Here, then, is my definition of JKD.

Lee discovered a set of universal principles that can be found in any art or any combination of arts. It is the perfect union of strategic principles, with the arts that best serve to actualize the intent of the principles, that defines JKD. There are six major principles:

Multicultural arts: "Having no way as way" means that one must recognize that no one country has a monopoly on knowledge.

Range: Combat exists within four ranges. By evaluating each art in terms of its effectiveness at one or more ranges, we tend to free ourselves from the obvious ethnocentrism associated with most styles.

Five ways of attack: There are five methods of offensively approaching an opponent. All attacks fit into one of the five ways.

Individual and instructor preference: The often-used phrase, "My truth is not your truth," stems from this principle.

Environment: The environment often dictates the skill to be employed. The boxer whose arms are bound or the kicker who attempts his techniques on ice will experience this principle first hand.

Absorb what is useful: Once a student understands and can incorporate the first five principles, then the sixth principle takes on new meaning.

JKD simply was Lee's conceptual framework. We can understand the term "conceptual framework" as being similar to a pair of glasses through which we examine the world. Let us suppose that our glasses have a green tint. Then everything we see looks green. In his own conceptual framework (lenses of his own prescription), Lee was greatly influenced by a need for reality in combat. Thus, when he looked at various arts through the conceptual framework of the six principles, he absorbed only the skills or methods he could see, or that he found personally useful.

We could take the same conceptual framework, give it to a person whose values centered around, let's say, pageantry, ritual, and social structure (as opposed to reality in combat), and we would end up with a highly evolved social structure for developing discipline and character. Our society, unfortunately, places more value on combat efficiency than on character development; thus, the "deity" status afforded Lee is easily understood. Dan Inosanto is among the few people capable of equally understanding, appreciating, and developing both value systems. Lee, on the other hand, appreciated primarily the values associated with combat. In my opinion, Dan exhibits greater wisdom, while Bruce (dead or alive) continues to exhibit greater attraction.

The six principles of JKD provide a workable understanding of the theoretical/philosophical definition of the term. However, I have found that JKD combines kali, Thai boxing, silat, and the various Jun Fan arts. This combination of arts is greatly influenced by JKD principle number four. Finally, JKD is a family. The social group that composes the JKD family shares common values that are discernable from other social groups of other arts.

Anyone who understands and can put to use the six principles will comprehend the theoretical/philosophical level of JKD. This understanding will invariably lead the participant to practice the JKD family arts (physical JKD) in conjunction with the family group (social JKD). As you can see, JKD can be defined and structured just as any other martial art. After 20 years of existence and practice, it's about time the art of Bruce Lee became known.

CHAPTER 2
Utilizing the Principles of JKD

The reader may perceive that at the time the *Inside Kung-Fu* editorial was published my thoughts regarding jeet kune do had not been developed fully. For example, I made no distinction in the editorial between original and conceptual JKD. To be sure, my definition of JKD in 1989 was that of conceptual JKD. As I continued to research and publish, I became acutely aware that the principles I had identified and the matrix I was developing were at a level never reached by Bruce Lee. He simply ran out of time.

Inside Karate editor John Soet, a known authority on Lee, provided this analogy regarding my principles of JKD: "The process of redactive criticism is exactly like reviewing a fight. A fight occurs, we do what we do instinctively, and then, after the fact, we go back over what we have done and analyze what happened . . . Only by backtracking through the source material available to us can we duplicate Lee's process (but not his product)."

Soet referred to my principles as redactive JKD. By following the scientific method I was, in effect, rewriting Lee's methodology. The principles of redactive JKD could be used to explain each of his "riddles." More importantly, redactive JKD can make an understanding of conceptual JKD more readily obtainable.

As I began to formulate the redactive JKD principles it

became apparent that the research strategy could be used to investigate any art. It is often said that, while much time and effort was put into developing the technology to fly man to the moon, the real reward was not in the final mission but in the knowledge derived from the research. Similarly, the identification of any principles with JKD was at one time a goal. However, once completed, the knowledge gained in the effort became considerably more satisfying.

Much of what I know about functional JKD I attribute to Joe Lewis. Lewis was without equal among the JKD students who trained with Lee. It may be said that while some original students focus on JKD concepts, others maintain that the modified wing chun best exemplifies JKD. Lewis concentrated his efforts on the Jun Fan kickboxing. Since the kickboxing was by far the most contact oriented (thus, the more realistic) practice in the JKD program, he faced little competition from other JKD students. To be sure, Lewis had to go outside the JKD family to find fighters for his kickboxing/full-contact karate title fights.

JKD: THE ORIGINAL BLOODFIST

If JKD has one major criticism, it is that it has never been tested in competition. Sure, the JKD advocates "talked a good talk," but could they "walk a good walk"? Bruce Lee refused to put his skill on the line in competition. Apparently, his students followed the same path.

Americans typically equate "the best" with sports competition. Some have claimed that JKD is not a proven art. However, upon closer inspection, we will see how it has, in fact, been tested in competition. The development of modern American kickboxing, what often is referred to as full-contact karate, was in its infancy nothing more than JKD.

The California Connection
Southern California has often been called the mecca of

American martial arts. The Californians are justifiably proud of their free spirits and innovative attitudes. It is no wonder, then, that Californians were the first to appreciate the idea of having two karate competitors, stripped to the waist and wearing boxing gloves, engage in a full-contact fight to the finish. On the night of January 17, 1970, martial arts history was made.

The scene was the legendary Long Beach, California, Municipal Auditorium. The talk at ringside that night was full of disbelief. After all, what kind of person would be willing to step into a ring and, in front of thousands of people, take the chance of being humiliated through injury or knockout? Most traditional karate men of the day agreed that the event was some kind of fake show. Why, a well-placed backfist, they had been taught, could rip off a man's head. A side kick could potentially cut a man in two. Now, what kind of a man would go into a ring and do this type of thing?

Greg Baines was one such man. A black Muslim who proudly stated his beliefs and did much to awaken a sense of pride among his brothers, Baines stood as the current California state heavyweight champion. His rippling muscles reflected years of concentrated effort. Weighing in at more than two hundred pounds, he was considered by most the best around. No man could take his challenge lightly.

His opponent was a young, blue-eyed, blond Adonis type. Sure, he sported a physique that would make Arnold Schwartzenegger take a second look, but Baines was there to hurt somebody—not to flex biceps. To add to his fearsome image, Baines wore a sardonic grin, a symbol of his religious conviction that he was on a mission to win. And while both men were known to have violent intents, it would take more than a recalcitrant attitude to win this fight.

The various masters who attended this original "bloodfist"-style event must have had a real chuckle over the way the young Adonis pranced around the ring. While Baines, the crowd's favorite, took a very traditional wide and deep stance, as if to invite his challenger to enter his powerful domain, the young Adonis—later to be celebrated as "the golden boy"—moved in and out as if on the balls of his feet. They all knew it was a wide and deep stance like Baines' that permitted the karateka to project the kind of power that could break bricks and stones—had not Mas Oyama and every Oriental master of the day proclaimed that this was so?

Yet in spite of popular beliefs, the young Adonis seemed to have no problem scoring points against the stationary Baines. Each time Baines would attempt a kick, his opponent would intercept the attack by stop-hitting the leg and firing off a hook or a double-hook combination. Against the often thrown karate-style punch, "the golden boy" would trap the strike and follow with a devastating strike of his own. By the end of the first round, the audience was stunned. This could not be karate that the blond muscle man was using. Sure, it was effective, but just wait until the next round. By then, surely the champion Baines would zero in and prove once and for all that the masters had been right. Hold your ground. Take your stance. The one-shot victory. This was traditional karate. This was what they had come to see.

But in the second round, Baines fared no better. Each time he would get set, the challenger would move. Each time he would return his opposite hand to his side, he would expose his head to a vicious hook. Baines had developed good karate skills, for sure. Unfortunately, the young Adonis, who by now was gaining crowd support, observed none of the traditional rules. His stances were light and quick, some said catlike. He would slip punches instead of blocking them. He kept his hands raised. And rather than lock out a punch, he snapped his fists in a whiplike manner.

Finally, in a movement previously unseen in karate competition, the young Adonis faked a technique, as if in slow motion. Then, in a supercharged flash, he changed leads, creating an opening for a double-hook combination. What art, what system, taught these skills? A fallen champion, Baines tumbled to the mat. The strikes had found their mark. No second chances.

Unlike fighters of today, Baines neither cried foul nor complained. He had been beaten. And while the new champion accepted the ovations of a standing audience, Baines retired from the ring. For some at ringside, and for far more who would hear of the young champion's exploits, Baines' retreat from the ring signaled the end of the glorious naiveté that dominated traditional martial arts.

No longer could one argue the unchallenged superiority of traditional karate, the most popular art of the day. For as the courageous Baines fell to the mat, years of uncontrolled boasting by karateka came to an end as well. Sure, there were those who ignored the event. Others argued that it wasn't really martial arts—they were, after all, wearing boxing gloves. And some even claimed that Baines was at fault. Yet Baines' was a most valiant effort. In the end, which came unexpectedly during the second round, it was not Baines' spirit that was to blame, nor did his strength fail him. It was the level of sophistication of his chosen art that had proven inefficient.

The young Adonis, now "the golden boy," went on to challenge the most feared karate competitors of his day. In ten consecutive matches, he knocked out each challenger during the first or second rounds. His art was jeet kune do.

Youthful readers may by now be dismissing this story as somewhat of a fairy tale. But it is fact. The young Adonis was Joe Lewis. In 1983, Lewis was voted by his peers—including Chuck Norris, Bill Wallace, Mike Stone, Steve Anderson, Keith Vitali, and others—as the "Greatest Fighter of All Time." Bruce Lee also referred to Lewis as the greatest fighter of his time. And while Lewis adopted an orthodox boxing method in later fights, his early kickboxing career was purely JKD.

JEET KUNE DO: THE LEWIS YEARS

Joe Lewis first met Bruce Lee in 1967. At the time, recalls Lewis, "he wanted to convince me that I should use my strong side forward." But Lewis didn't believe in changing his stance at the time. By 1970, however, he had become a full-time Lee protégé who tested out JKD theories in tournament competition.

According to Lewis, Lee's overall theme was simplicity. While Lee maintained his own chosen style, which was of no interest to Lewis, he integrated other arts into his practice. The end result was often more important than the origin of the style. Lee explained to Lewis that JKD was the way of the intercepting fist. Lee, says Lewis, "liked to use the term 'thusness.'" The "thusness" of the technique referred to its success, not its practice or attempt. Lee conjectured that an opponent's attack dictated the potential counters. One simply performs a skill based on the energy of the attack. After all, fighting, according to Lee, was simply a game of quick reactions. JKD, then, was "a philosophical concept applied to fighting principles," says Lewis. Lewis, who outweighed Lee by more than sixty pounds, believed that Lee could do exactly what he said he could. "Bruce could make JKD work because he had the right attitude, the physical ability, the mentality, and philosophy," he says. "He could put it all together."

Lee had two types of students—his special students whom he taught privately and his general workout buddies who comprised his classes for group lessons. Lewis worked out privately with Lee on Wednesdays during the late '60s and early '70s. According to Lewis, "We would begin each lesson with a general discussion of philosophy, and we would review fighting tapes with Jack Dempsey or Mohammed Ali in them." In studying the films, they would try to incorporate two principles—closing the gap and mobility. The method was to view the tapes repeatedly in order to get the image of the perfect technique into their minds. Says Lewis, "Lee could convince you that you could do what he was telling you you could do."

Of course, Lewis worked out up to eight hours a day. As he told one reporter, his workouts consisted of skill repetition and sparring. There was no talk or rest—just hard work. Lewis and Lee shared the belief in hard work. Both enjoyed enviable physiques as a by-product of their dedication to fitness.

The workout routines varied, ranging from learning independent motion in front of a mirror to focus glove training. Within the first year, Lewis had become virtually unbeatable in competition. Not only did he win eleven straight point tournaments, he enjoyed similar success in kickboxing. Regarding his work with Lee, Lewis notes that Lee was fond of the statement, "Look at a finger pointing to the moon. Don't take the finger to be the moon." What he showed Lewis about JKD was a special insight not shared with other JKD devotees.

Obviously, Lewis has been the most successful (if not the only) competitive fighter in the JKD camp. Yet he has shied away from any identification with JKD. For nearly a decade, I studied closely with Lewis the concepts of JKD, with emphasis on the (Jun Fan) kickboxing. As I mentioned earlier, Lewis concentrated on the science of fighting. Other JKD practitioners have concentrated on the art of technique development. Lewis applied JKD; others have taught it. There is a different message to be learned from each group. As junfanologists, there is no right or wrong group—just knowledge to be gained.

I believe Lewis represents the essence of the Lee style of fighting (kickboxing method). His strategy and training methods have been greatly advanced since Lee's death in 1973. Lewis and I coauthored the following article, entitled "Beyond the Angles of Attack" (originally published in the July 1988 issue of *Black Belt*).

▼

BEYOND THE ANGLES OF ATTACK

When Joe Lewis introduced the theory of angular attack in the early 1970s, it was heralded as the most advanced technical series of its day. Champion fighters Bill Wallace, Jeff Smith, Steve Anderson, Keith Vitali, Howard Jackson, and others claimed that Lewis' principles greatly enhanced their ability to approach opponents in competition. (The term "angle" is used in this case to imply a method or approach and should not be confused with a geometric measurement.)

Lewis has never been shy about admitting that when he first heard the term "angles of attack" from Lee in 1968, he too had a problem understanding it. Lee, of course, borrowed the strategy from fencing. In the various jeet kune do (way of the stopping fist) manuals, you'll notice that Lee (or his students) employs the phrase "five ways of attack."

Lee's personal fighting system called for use of the strong side forward. Thus, like the fencer, he used his strong side to attack his opponent. He viewed the "stop-hit," another fencing term, as a higher order of combat which, in part, gave rise to the concept of JKD. Some experts have maintained that the key to understanding Lee's interpretation is to see that, utilizing the strong-side-forward method, he attempted to translate weapons strategy in terms of empty-hand defense. When you only have one weapon, as with the fencer, you of course want to keep the strong side (weapon) out in front.

Lewis maintains that Lee's interest in fencing methods gave rise to the use of independent motion in karate competition. After working with Lee, Lewis won a number of tournaments (bear in mind that Lewis was declared a national champion as early as 1966) with the strong-side-forward strategy. However, after a year of personal exchange with Lee (and perhaps motivated by Lee's analytical methodology), Lewis began interpreting the angles of attack not as a method of fencing without a foil, but as a method of offensively approaching an opponent without the fencing mentality. Lewis' system or adaptation was developed for karate competition. It has since been found effective for any form of unarmed combat.

One of the first changes Lewis made was to put the strong side back instead of forward. Boxers, for example, lead with the weaker side to set up a knockout strike from the stronger side. Many schools of karate and tae kwon do practice kicking and punching from the reverse side to insure maximum power and velocity. Following is Lewis' entire system of angular attack.

Lewis' Original Five Angles of Attack

The five angles of attack are methods of offensive footwork utilized in approaching an opponent. The first method is called "direct angular attack" and is employed by striking directly at the opponent. Most practitioners rely primarily on the direct attack as the major means of delivering a kick, punch, elbow, or knee strike, etc. Should the direct attack not hit its target, one could try again or vary the angle (method of approach) of the attack.

The second angle of attack incorporates the use of a fake. For example, one may fake a kick to hit the opponent with a punch. This angle is called an "indirect angular attack."

"Combination angular attack" represents the third method of offensively approaching an opponent. Combination simply means using any two angles of attack in conjunction. For example, a fighter may use several direct attacks in combination to successfully hit his opponent.

The fourth angle of attack, "immobilization," implies that one immobilizes the opponent's offense while delivering his own attack. Most karate and tae kwon do competitors have at one time or another grabbed an opponent's sleeve or pant leg and, while holding or, in this case, immobilizing the opponent's arm or leg, delivered an

The author, with JKD kickboxing mentor and world karate champion Joe Lewis, demonstrates early JKD training methods as taught by Bruce Lee. In Figure 7, against a stationary opponent, Lewis (right) traps the forward hand (Figure 8) and strikes with a forward hook (Figure 9).

Figure 7

Figure 8

Figure 9

A favorite Lee training routine was to trap the forward hand (Figure 10) and check, or immobilize, the lead leg (Figure 11), setting up a power side kick (Figure 12).

Figure 10

Figure 11

Figure 12

A common Lee-style training method was to trap the forward hand (Figure 13) and complete the motion with a straight punch (Figure 14). Lee preferred the vertical punch over the commonly practiced turnover punch.

Figure 13

Figure 14

attack. This is one of the most commonly used methods.

Finally, "broken rhythm angular attack" employs a variance in speed or direction as a means of approaching the opponent. Although broken rhythm should be the exclusive domain of the most advanced practitioners, it is often successfully used, albeit unknowingly, by the beginner. The fact is that beginners and experts show an ability to deliver strikes that seemingly change speed and/or direction in midair. Or the fighter advances in such a fashion as to be out of position for your attack but in perfect position to hit you. Imagine starting a punch in slow speed. As your opponent adjusts to the same slow speed, you quickly speed up the technique. Before your opponent has time to react to the

Figure 15

Here, Lewis utilizes indirect attack by completing a hip fake (Figure 15) followed by a vertical punch (Figure 16). A leg-check immobilization (Figure 17) is a natural follow-up, which sets up the round kick (Figures 18 and 19), which Lee called a hook kick since it followed the same path as the boxer's hook punch.

Figure 16

Figure 17

Figure 18

Figure 19

new speed, he has been hit. You have, in effect, successfully delivered an attack using broken rhythm angular attack.

Of course, you cannot expect every opponent to react in the same manner. Defensively, an opponent will react in one of three ways: he will either block, move away, or jam your attack. Matching the three types of defensive footwork with the five types of offensive footwork provides a martial artist with an advanced formula for performing any system.

Beyond Angular Attack

The angular attack theory is the highest order of understanding for the application of any offensive technique. However, the

Here, Lewis again applies a hip fake (Figure 20) and a vertical punch combination (Figure 21), following with the reverse punch in Figure 22. Lee and Lewis would spend hours perfecting feigning techniques to set up attacks.

Figure 20

Figure 21

Figure 22

In Figure 23, Lewis shuffles in and feigns a low attack (indirect angular attack). As his opponent reacts in Figure 24, Lewis traps the forward arm (immobilization) and completes a reverse punch (Figure 25) and elbow strike (Figure 26). In actual practice sessions, Lewis and Lee often wore gloves and shin protectors since many routines incorporated low kicks.

Figure 23

Figure 24

Figure 25

Figure 26

Figure 27

A favorite routine of Lee's was low kick setup (Figure 27), followed by a double hook punch (Figures 28-31).

Figure 28

37

Figure 29

Figure 30

Figure 31

practitioner's ability to be successful can be enhanced or hampered by the type of technique used. Direct attacks, for example, are at times more successful in arts incorporating independent motion. Arm and leg immobilization is similarly more clearly understood by practitioners of arts that employ advanced trapping techniques.

"Selective technique variation" denotes a system for adopting specific techniques based on the potential of those maneuvers for enhancing angular attack. It is used to supplement your system and improve your chances for effectiveness at kicking, punching, and grappling ranges.

Selective technique variation is employed only to enhance your skills and should not be viewed as a goal in and of itself. Rather, the goal is to more readily express the validity of the angular attack methodology.

It should also be understood that learning techniques simply for the sake of knowing techniques is not a process of selective technique variation. The boxer who learns kicking skills or the karateka (karate stylist) who can perform boxing footwork can be identified with the selective technique variation method only when the moves are used during the successful performance of angular attack. Techniques are always chosen on the basis of their ability to increase performance, not because it has become fashionable to mix styles.

Far too many martial artists judge techniques on their source rather than on effectiveness. For example, many karate and tae kwon do practitioners attempt to negate the validity of boxing because they have identified the art with some of the poorly performed boxing matches they have seen. Practitioners of some Korean systems often refuse to consider the value of Japanese karate kicks, not because they don't work, but because the source is Japanese. Each martial art employs techniques and other skills that can be of value. No culture has a monopoly on martial arts knowledge. There is no one best system that will work for everyone. A practitioner should employ skills or techniques based on function, not on historical source.

Many karate and tae kwon do fighters do not use immobilization-angular attacks because their arts fail to incorporate trapping skills found in arts like wing chun and kali. Understanding angular attack means recognizing the fact that other arts present alternative techniques that could greatly enhance one's ability to perform this fighting method.

Simply having more techniques is not the answer, however. Some students attempt to collect so many techniques from so many martial arts that they ultimately master none. Having knowledge of so many techniques without an understanding of the five ways of delivering them in an offensive manner would limit even the most advanced student.

Integrating new physical methods does not destroy a style. All martial arts were originally developed by combining the skills available at the time of their creation. Different names, dates, countries, religions, and values are the significant components of a style. Physical skills have always varied and have changed to reflect the needs of the society in which they were used. Modern skills can be employed without significantly changing an appreciation for historical founders, their values and beliefs, or other forms of identifying with a particular style.

Some martial artists prefer the experience of performing classical skills in the same manner in which they were originally developed. These traditional practitioners can incorporate basic angular attack theory without in any way altering their styles. Remember, these methods have always existed and have been used throughout centuries of combat.

Those individuals who prefer to go beyond the angles of attack will find that selective technique variation will increase their chances for success in the modern martial arts arena. Whether you are concentrating on tournaments or street defense, selective technique variation, coupled with the theory of angular attack, will insure measurable success.

The responses to the "Beyond the Angles of Attack" article were quite favorable. During this same time period, my book, *In Search of The Ultimate Martial Art: The Jeet Kune Do Experience,* was receiving excellent reviews. The stage was set to approach *Black Belt* magazine readers with my redactive JKD principles. Unlike so many who had simply glorified the mystique surrounding Bruce Lee, I was ready to admit publicly that Lee had produced an unfinished art. But how would the readers respond? Here is the article that I called "Solving the Riddle of Jeet Kune Do,"which appeared in the April 1989 issue of *Black Belt.*

▼

SOLVING THE RIDDLE OF JEET KUNE DO

In 1967 Bruce Lee developed a combat concept called jeet kune do. This fighting theory has been taught, written about, photographed, and argued over for more than 20 years, yet it never has been objectively defined. This lack of definition has proven to be a major source of confusion for those who teach and those who try to learn an art with no boundaries.

JKD often is called the "style of no style," or "using no way as the way." It has been defined as "the way of the intercepting fist" and as a select combination of twenty-six arts. One martial artist concluded that JKD was simply Lee's personal art and either you knew it or you didn't, and that was that! These statements are not definitions; they are riddles intended to maintain an aura through confusion.

The fact is that, to the general public and the average martial arts enthusiast, to learn JKD means that you will somehow develop Lee's skill. And to teach JKD implies that the instructor has Lee's skills and can pass them on to the student. Thus, JKD's attraction has been due not so much to the art itself but the identification of the art with Lee.

By using riddles instead of concrete definitions, anyone, certified or not, has the opportunity to quote the riddle and play the role of "holder of Lee's skills." It is no wonder that even those who are certified to teach JKD often cannot give a reasonable definition of the art.

Going beyond angles of attack strategy involves incorporating skills of other arts that best exemplify the principles employed. In this sequence, Beasley incorporates an aikido-like entry in Figure 32, followed in Figure 33 by a bicep destruction identified with kali to set up a karate-style round kick (Figure 34).

Figure 32

Figure 33

Figure 34

In this sequence, Beasley redirects the opponent's attack (Figure 35) and shuffles to the right (Figure 36) to confuse the opponent before setting up the round kick in Figure 37 and following with destruction in Figures 38 and 39.

Figure 35

Figure 36

Figure 37

Figure 38

Figure 39

It is a sociological fact that, more often than not, those things that are held to be most important to an individual or group often are the most difficult to objectively define. These closely guarded truths can, in most cases, be defined only in terms of emotions. For this reason, it often is said that one cannot define JKD; one only can experience it. Thus, the riddles of JKD, when used by practitioners, may be viewed as an attempt to emotionally rather than objectively define a subject that previously has been experienced and not examined. To prove the existence of JKD, we must "blindly follow" a concept based on the emotionally charged premise that Lee developed an art that can be taught.

The Science of Inquiry

In the movie "Predator," a group of combat specialists led by Arnold Schwartzenegger was being stalked and killed off by an alien being. The alien predator, in the first part of the movie, could not be heard or seen; it only could be "experienced" through the emotions (in this case, fear). In his search for concrete traces of the existence of the predator, one member of the team saw what appeared to be blood. Schwartzenneger, using a method of scientific inquiry, reasoned that, "If it bleeds, we can kill it." And indeed he did.

Using this same method of inquiry, we too can propose a question. If JKD exists, we can define it. If, on the other hand, it died with Lee, we can determine that as well.

Just as one may need specialized equipment for combating a predator, martial artists must employ specialized methods in their struggle to combat the prevalence of misinformation. As long as the predator was defined in terms of emotion (fear), no one could prove it existed. And if JKD continues to be defined in terms of emotional riddles (based on unquestioned respect), it will be difficult to prove it exists or does not exist. Moreover, it will be difficult to prove who is and who is not teaching or practicing JKD. There will of course be signs. The predator left dead bodies everywhere which, in turn, increased the emotionally based belief that something killed them. But what? Lee left movies in which he exhibited phenomenal skills in what would have to be called pretend battles. In watching Lee, one invariably develops the emotion of respect.

Accounts of his life suggest that Lee was very adamant about the superiority of his fighting style. Perhaps it was this emotional constraint that inhibited him from objectively preparing a program for study. In addition to the various JKD riddles coined by Lee and others, there are other bodies of information. There is Ohara Publications' *Tao of Jeet Kune Do*, various "certified" instructors, a film library, eyewitness accounts, and volumes of literature about JKD. During any given weekend, dozens of JKD classes or seminars are being taught. Now that we know where to

While the previous two routines may best be identified with JKD concepts methods, this one demonstrates an original JKD-style counter utilizing a low-leg kick (Figure 40), followed by trapping (Figure 41) and a leg sweep (Figure 42) for the takedown (Figure 43).

Figure 40

Figure 41

look, we must first prepare a method for data acquisition.

In view of the fact that JKD has yet to be adequately defined, the study lends itself to qualitative analysis. Techniques of participant observation, interviewing, and content analysis provide the proper methodology for collecting data in defining JKD.

Defining Jeet Kune Do

The term "conceptual framework" is often used to denote a method of observing a phenomenon. We can compare a conceptual framework to a pair of glasses. If we put on a pair of glasses with green lenses, everything we see will have a green tint. Glasses, of course, come in different colors as well as different

Figure 42

Figure 43

prescriptions. To be able to best see through a pair of glasses, we must have the proper prescription.

Every martial art maintains a conceptual framework based on the value system of its creator. If we observed two fighters, based on the values we have learned in the study of shotokan karate, for example, we would no doubt look for the straight lines of combat and the victorious character of the participants. Just as shotokan founder Gichin Funakoshi stressed character development in real life, the conceptual framework for his art stresses a recognition of the perfection of character. To understand Funakoshi's karate, we must wear the glasses of his prescription. Many have successfully tried.

To see JKD, we must wear the prescription lenses of Lee. Defining JKD requires that we understand the philosophical/theoretical, the physical, and the social components that characterize the system. On the philosophical and theoretical level, JKD is simply Lee's conceptual framework. Just as we must know a particular prescription to correctly cut and grind a lens so that we can properly see, we must identify the proper prescription of Lee so we can see more clearly the components that comprise JKD.

The methodology employed in this study has resulted in the identification of six principles that define philosophical and theoretical JKD. We know from all accounts that Lee valued combat efficiency above all other attributes awarded to various martial arts. As a result, his framework stems from those principles that could best actualize the theme of reality in combat. Following are the six principles.

Multicultural arts: Remember that the principles are brought to life through the performance of technique. If there is a single quality that virtually all modern JKD practitioners demonstrate, it is the understanding of Filipino, Thai, Chinese, Western, and, more recently, Indonesian arts. We can identify the physical performance trait as resulting from an understanding of the principle of multicultural arts.

Since no one country has a monopoly on knowledge, it behooves the prudent student to develop expertise in skills to be used in all four fighting ranges (kicking, punching, trapping, and grappling), without regard to cultural restraints. A student of JKD principles is not bound by the skills of only one art. The individual may flow from a wing chun trap to a Thai boxing elbow (or any other economical combination) as the principle of multicultural arts is used.

Range: A major component of the conceptual framework that is JKD is the principle of range, or what is often called "fighting distance." By evaluating each art in terms of its effectiveness at one or more of the four combat ranges, we tend to free ourselves of the ethnocentrism associated with most styles. When we combine the multicultural concept with an understanding of the principle of range or distance, we can begin to see the pattern of JKD. In physical performance, the student of these two JKD principles is, in fact, not bound by style, but simply expresses the necessity of the moment. In kicking range, one simply kicks. Specific styles may go to extremes in identifying each kick. How to best place the foot, how to effectively use the proper kiai (yell), and at what angle and height the hands should be placed are the prerequisites of style and should be of minimal concern to the JKD practitioner.

Five ways of attack: There are five methods of offensively approaching an opponent. A Lee student often identified with promoting the use of angles of attack is Joe Lewis. (While Lewis is not typically identified as a member of the JKD family, he nevertheless exemplifies various JKD principles.) The methods of both Lee and Lewis focus on direct, indirect, combination, immobilization, and rhythm-disruption attacks. The principle of angles or ways of attack encompasses all forms of combat.

Individual and instructor preference: The often-used phrase, "My truth is not your truth," stems from the principles of individual and instructor preference. While Lee chose to interpret JKD principles in terms of his cultural art of Chinese wing chun, Dan Inosanto feels more at home with his own cultural art of Filipino kali. Larry Hartsell, on the other hand, is the appointed leader of JKD grappling methods. While each artist shares the principles of JKD, the interpretation depends largely on their individual preferences. If the reader feels, for example, most comfortable at punching range, his range of combat naturally will concentrate on those lines.

A problem comes into play when, for instance, a short, stubby man is made to perform in kicking range even though his natural strength may well be at punching or grappling range. In seeking the "truth," the student must understand that instructors almost always promote their personal values. The instructor's values may be similar to or different from the student's values. If individual and instructor values differ substantially, one would be best advised to seek another teacher, art, or both.

Environment: To illustrate the principle of environment, Inosanto often uses the simile of the grenade, the knife, and the phone booth. When asked which is the better weapon, the knife or the grenade, one might reply that the grenade is better because it has greater power and range. In a foxhole, of course, the grenade would be preferred. However, if one were forced into combat in a phone booth, would not the knife be the weapon of choice? The environment often dictates the skills to be used.

We all have heard by now the example of the tae kwon do practitioner attempting to perform his high kicks on slippery ice or jungle mud. If you have invested all of your time in perfecting a particular skill, the environment may well aid in your defeat. Some of the skills used in a boxing ring or on a karate tournament floor should no doubt be adjusted to more closely facilitate their use in the street environment.

Absorb what is useful: Once the student understands and can utilize the first five principles of JKD, the sixth principle, "Absorb what is useful," takes on new meaning. Otherwise, it is simply a nebulous phrase, albeit an enticing one. By investigating multicultural arts, experiencing the ways of attack, appreciating the importance of instructor and individual preference, and recognizing the restraints of the environment and range, one should be more adept at incorporating techniques into a system that has the potential to flow naturally.

For example, it is not difficult to flow from a wing chun lop sao (trap) to a boxing hook. However, it is difficult (due to the fact that the combination fails to observe the concept of economy of motion) to use a karateka's high block with a boxer's jab. Again, the matching of techniques into a sense of flow and economy of motion, and taking into consideration personal preference to, in effect, "absorb what is useful" are best actualized by the student who fully comprehends the principles of multicultural arts, range, and environment.

Lee developed JKD as a conceptual framework to facilitate solving the problems of personal combat. The components of the JKD conceptual framework include the six major principles outlined previously, as well as several lesser tenets that are most concerned with "tool" development. Economy of motion, attribute development, and flow are representative of these technique-oriented principles.

On the physical level, modern JKD practitioners tend to combine the original Jun Fan (Bruce Lee) arts of wing chun and Jun Fan kickboxing with the Inosanto-influenced arts of kali, muay thai, and pentjak-silat. It would be safe to say that the current crop of JKD practitioners can be identified by their strong prefer-ence for kali and other support systems. Finally, on the social level, JKD is, as Inosanto put it, "family." It would seem that those identified as being in the JKD family are recognized by oth-ers within the family.

Realistically, one could employ the JKD conceptual frame-work (theoretical and philosophical JKD) independently from the JKD "family arts" (social and physical JKD) classifications. However, the realistic use of the conceptual framework invari-ably leads one to study the "family arts." In so doing, one gains both a higher understanding of the principles and the recognition as a member of the family.

In the final analysis, we may reasonably conclude that JKD does, in fact, exist. JKD is a conceptual framework composed of the six major principles currently demonstrated through the physical skills selected by the JKD group. It should be stressed that the principles of JKD exist independently of any style, group, or individual. Whether we call them principles of JKD or by some other name is not important.

Moreover, according to principle number four, the interpreta-tion of JKD may take the form of any art or combination of arts. And while physical and social JKD have been and will continue to be directed by the JKD family, theoretical JKD—the art of six principles—knows no boundaries.

CHAPTER 3
The Matrix

Any scientist will tell you that research is never an end. It is merely a beginning. The research developed for the "riddle" article resulted in the concept of the jeet kune do matrix. The matrix is a most important contribution to redactive JKD methodology. One can understand JKD as it is formulated through the matrix. As one comprehends the multicultural arts principle and the concept of range, the foundations of redactive JKD can be readily recognized. The following article on the JKD matrix first appeared in the April 1989 issue of *Inside Kung-Fu*. At the time, I considered it my most important effort.

▼

THE JKD MATRIX
When Bruce Lee died in 1973 the martial arts world was stunned. It's fair to say that Lee didn't officially "arrive" on the martial arts scene until that unforgettable demonstration in 1964 at the Long Beach Internationals. By 1967 he had recognized a method of developing a martial arts system which he called jeet kune do. Six years later he was dead.

Most martial artists agree that one would be hard-pressed to fully develop a system in six years. Those martial artists would be right. JKD wasn't fully developed during those six years. A formula, a method of understanding the parameters of the system, was never fully conceptualized, at least not to the point of being chronicled.

Instead, JKD was, for those not privileged to associate with JKD "family members," kept alive through various riddles that spoke of an art as yet undefined. On the theoretical level, JKD exists as an unrefined concept of a "style of all styles," as an art that knows no boundaries. At first glance it would be easy to dismiss this whole issue of JKD as a fantasy art that died with its creator. Many have chosen this path.

Yet we cannot deny that there exists a group of individuals who actually trained with Lee and have kept his teachings alive through seminars and demonstrations. Something called JKD undoubtedly exists, but after fifteen years of reading about it, writing about it, and watching it, has anyone reasonably defined it? It can be taught, but can it be learned? At times one could be doing JKD; at other times, one is simply performing techniques from a style.

What does it mean to say that sometimes my JKD resembles kali while at other times it appears to be muay thai? To follow *Inside Kung-Fu* editor Dave Cater's controversial, yet valid, argument ("Editorial," August 1988), if the performer can't be sure of what he is performing, how then can the viewer be sure of what he is viewing?

Defining JKD

To answer these questions we must position JKD into understandable categories. We can be sure that JKD exists on a physical level. Modern JKD practitioners and instructors tend to combine the original Jun Fan arts of wing chun and Jun Fan kickboxing with the Dan Inosanto-influenced arts of kali, muay thai, and silat.

In addition to physical reality, JKD exists on a social level. As Inosanto often says, "JKD is family." Members of the JKD family have an established line of entry stemming from Lee, Inosanto, or a number of other family-endorsed instructors. Those identified as being in the JKD family are recognized by others within the family. Thus, we can easily define JKD in terms of a physical JKD

(Jun Fan wing chun, Inosanto-influenced kali, muay thai, silat, etc.) and a social JKD (members of the JKD family).

There is, however, a third definition that we'll call "theoretical" JKD. On the theoretical level JKD exists as a set of principles that influence the development of a martial arts system. Lee, like everyone (including Gogen Yamaguchi, Chojun Miyagi, Gichin Funakoshi, Inosanto, and just about anyone else you can name), had a particular method of looking at martial arts. We'll call this method a conceptual framework.

A conceptual framework may be likened to a lens in a pair of glasses. If the lens is blue, the images that we see will have a blue tint. Lee's lenses, his glasses, were composed of concepts and values he attached to fighting arts. We know, for example, that Lee stressed reality in combat. Lee preferred arts that could justify economy of motion. We also know that he valued arts not so much for their cultural origins (styles) as for their utility in the combat arena. To Lee, arts were of value only when they could be used within grappling, kicking, and punching ranges.

By way of comparison, we also might note that the conceptual framework of Funakoshi, for example, was influenced or prescribed by his individual values. Funakoshi stressed that a martial art should become a vehicle for character development. Funakoshi, unlike Lee, valued not the combat efficiency of an art (the victory of defeat), but the manner in which the art enhanced the development of one's character. From all accounts Lee wasn't very interested in the perfection of his own character; he was known to be temperamental and high-strung. Comparing the two founders should make it easier to understand the meaning of a conceptual framework and how it can be compared to a pair of glasses through which we can view our own world.

Lee's conceptual framework varies considerably from the conceptual framework of a karate master, a tae kwon do expert, or a muay thai champion. Each individual, in his own way, carries his own preferences, values, and concepts that reflect his own interpretations of what the individual prefers in a martial art.

The six principles of theoretical JKD could be placed in a

JKD concepts utilize arts which are most productive at specific ranges, regardless of cultural indications. The choice of techniques should be based on what works and not on the limitations of a specific style. In this first defense, the author draws on a silat-like elbow entry (Figure 44) with a leg takedown (Figures 45 and 46) and reposition (Figure 47).

Figure 44

Figure 45

matrix in which the full parameters of the concept could be defined. I'm not sure that anyone is capable of completing the total matrix. A total matrix would have to include, under the heading of multicultural arts, a listing of every conceivable art from every country. A total matrix might well encompass several hundred entries. We've been told that Lee included twenty-seven arts in his personal matrix. And, according to one JKD/kali instructor, "On the average, 5 to 10 percent of each system was used within the JKD framework. In certain cases, just training methods or fighting theories were utilized." Until now, few individuals have envisioned the full potential of theoretical JKD. Some, no doubt, would argue that we have, in our "ivory

Note that while most JKD practitioners shun uniforms, preferring street clothes (which in turn become their uniforms), the author is not burdened by this limitation.

Figure 46

Figure 47

tower," taken theoretical JKD beyond the limits of reality.

It is hoped that the reader will develop his JKD matrix using at least three of the JKD principles. Perhaps someone will advance the simple matrix provided herein to a more sophisticated level. At minimum, the reader can more clearly visualize the meaning of theoretical JKD through use of the matrix, thus experiencing a more complete understanding of the physical, social, and theoretical ramifications of Bruce Lee's conceptual framework.

The Matrix for Redactive JKD

There are six principles in redactive jeet kune do that should be considered by competent instructors who intend to develop

Against the reverse punch (Figure 48), the author chooses a karate-style block followed by a wing chun-like eye strike (Figure 49), a technique that Bruce Lee often demonstrated. To finish the technique, a jujutsu-like arm manipulation (Figure 50) is followed by a knee strike (Figure 51). Note that the techniques flow naturally. In retrospect, certain techniques are typically identified with different styles of martial arts, i.e., the arm bend with jujutsu, the eye strike with wing chun. Thus, the JKD presentation has no boundaries in that any art may be represented. It should also be noted that at no time is the performer simply wing chun, karate, etc. Rather, to borrow a phrase Bruce Lee often used, the "thusness" of the response is simply to respond without limitation. The choice of skills and the manner in which one performs them become an individual response to an opponent's energy (attack).

Figure 48

Figure 49

Figure 50

In other words, my art becomes your art. If your attack is in kicking range, my art looks like a kicking art. If you attack in grappling range, my art appears to be a grappling art.

Figure 51

gradually the physical skills of their respective systems. Once again, the principles are:

Multicultural arts: Since no one has a monopoly on knowledge, it behooves the prudent student to develop expertise in skills to be used in all four fighting ranges (kicking, punching, trapping, and grappling) without the bounds of cultural restraints. Instructors must, without bias, supplement their karate and tae kwon do systems to cover not only kicking but punching, trapping, and grappling ranges. Ancient and modern wisdom suggests that we seek out instructors, regardless of style, who specialize in each range so that we can develop our own level of competence.

Range: All combat is governed by the principle of range, or fighting distance. One of the first concepts taught in a Joe Lewis seminar is that the person who controls his distance controls the fight. If one's preferred range is kicking distance, then the other ranges must be supplemented to strengthen combative efficiency.

Five ways of attack: There are five methods of offensively approaching an opponent. These methods are: direct, indirect, combination, immobilization, and rhythm-disruption attacks. The principles of angles or ways of attack encompass all forms of combat.

Individual and instructor preference: The often-used phrase "My truth is not your truth" stems from the principles of individual and instructor preference. Based on individual needs and abili-

To understand JKD concepts is not to compare arts or skills as part of a performance. The end result is more important than the interpretation of the skill. In this sequence the author intercepts a straight punch with a redirection technique found in Chinese, Filipino, and Japanese arts (Figure 52). In Figure 53 the opponent is drawn into the finger strike.

Figure 52

Figure 53

ties, we tend to focus our skills in certain areas. I, for example, appreciate the atmosphere of the most traditional of karate dojos. However, in practice I prefer the physical high of a sophisticated kickboxing match. Yet in self-defense I have a preference for successful psychological maneuvers with a backup of pressure-point control. We should each seek to identify our personal preferences based on variety and then focus our skills in preferred and functional areas.

Environment: Remember that all combative forms reflect, to an extent, a preferred social, political, and structural environment. Tae kwon do, it is so often said, is least efficient in the structured environment of an ice-covered pond. The Zulu shield of the

Figure 54

Because the opponent's energy is moving forward, the author allows him to continue his forward movement while disrupting the forward arm (Figure 54) and maneuvering the opponent into a shoulder lock (Figures 55 and 56).

Figure 55

Figure 56

Again, the opponent dictates the technique (your attack becomes my attack). Because the opponent fails to adjust and continues forward, Beasley moves into an aiki jujutsu-type arm throw (Figures 57 and 58).

Figure 57

Figure 58

Figure 59

Figure 60

Figures 59-64 demonstrate how the author's attack (response) is dictated by the opponent's intent. In this sequence the author is met with sufficient forward pressure so that, when redirected, the opponent's energy causes him to be off-balanced (an aikido-like move) and thrown to the ground.

Figure 61

Figure 62

In this case a principle found in the Japanese art of aikido is easily applied for success. Experience each art in that there is a lesson to be learned from each country.

Figure 63

Figure 64

Ngumi people of South Africa was of great use against other African fighters but found a weakness against the European Martini-Henry rifle. The power of a .44 magnum is of limited use against the scope-sighted rifle at a thousand yards. And the karateka's empty hands are of diminished value in the boxer's ring or on the grappler's mat. Understanding the limitations of a "fixed" system or technique and not being bound by these limitations are of common concern.

"Absorb what is useful": Once the practitioner understands and can utilize the first five principles of redactive JKD, the sixth principle, "Absorb what is useful," takes on new meaning. By investigating multicultural arts, experiencing the ways of attack, appre-

ciating the importance of instructor and individual preference, and recognizing the restraints of the environment and range, one can be more adept at incorporating techniques into a system that has the potential to naturally flow.

The six principles of redactive JKD can be more easily understood when positioned in a matrix. A simple redactive JKD matrix can be developed to identify the strengths, weaknesses, preferences, and parameters (limitations) of any martial artist. We can construct a simple matrix in the following manner:

1. In the far left column, list the arts you have studied along with their nationalities.

2. In the next four columns, identify the "preferred range" for each art listed in part one.

3. In the final column, place the numbers 1, 2, or 3 to indicate your "individual preference" (1 being the highest preference).

Remember, this is a simple matrix for immediate use. A more detailed matrix can be constructed after a full understanding of redactive JKD theory has been developed.

Keep in mind that the original JKD concept is a philosophy that an individual should prepare for combat in a variety of ranges and environments utilizing the most economical methods while being unrestricted by national or cultural bias. Redactive JKD intends to move from the philosophical to the theoretical level as principles of combat are used as pragmatic components of the matrix. After completing the redactive JKD matrix, you should have a better understanding of your system and your ability to defend yourself in a variety of situations.

Multicultural arts: List arts under the following headings: Japanese, Korean, Filipino, Chinese, American, Thai, etc.

Personal preference: Place 1, 2, or 3 beside each entry, with 1 being a major preference.

Range: Is the art more functional for you at kicking, punching, trapping, or grappling range?

Perhaps no other JKD article has received as much atten-

Multicultural Arts—List arts under the following headings: Japanese, Korean, Filipino, Chinese, American, Thai, etc.

Personal Preference—Place 1, 2, or 3 beside each entry with one being a major preference.

Range—Is the art more functional for you at kicking, punching, trapping, or grappling range?

	K	P	T	G	
Japanese					
Karate	k				2
Jujutsu				g	2
Aikido				g	3
Korean					
Tae kwon do	k				2
Filipino					
Kali			t		2
Chinese					
Wing chun			t		3
American					
Boxing		p	t		1
Wrestling				g	3
Thai					
Muay Thai	k		t		2

* The numbers to the right represent the author's personal matrix.

tion as the "Matrix." Practitioners from across the country (including JKD instructors) phoned or wrote to assure me that, perhaps for the first time, the concept of JKD was becoming clear. Unfortunately, understanding the matrix would allow some individuals to disregard their own arts in favor of utilizing arts that could best be used to complete the matrix.

It is my view that the most important product of a martial art is the provision of positive self-esteem, discipline, and character development. Our society tends to value self-defense ability and ignore character development. The article "Redactive JKD and Classical Karate," which first appeared in the March 1990 issue of *Inside Karate*, was intended to promote the idea that character development is equally important to the development of redactive JKD.

▼

REDACTIVE JEET KUNE DO AND CLASSICAL KARATE

Ethnocentrism is not an appealing word. It is a term often used by social scientists to explain how certain groups develop elaborate, self-flattering explanations for suggesting that their group is somehow superior to others. Just as there is no significant proof that one race is superior to another, there exists no conclusive evidence to support the belief that a particular martial art is superior to others.

All martial arts provide experience and individual preferences passed on by the arts' creators. These preferences are in turn affected by the cultural constraints knowingly or otherwise presented by the arts' founders. Yet there are many martial artists who take pride in going about pontificating on how they alone possess a superior philosophy, theory, or physical skills and how others should recognize their inferior status. Ethnocentrism is alive and doing well in the martial arts.

There Is No "Best"

We may often hear that this person, that country, or this art

In this sequence the opponent uses a straight punch followed by a right cross in rapid fire. The author uses a boxing-style check (Figure 65) followed by a wing chun-like elbow redirection (Figure 66), which sets up a forearm (Figures 67 and 68) and reverse forearm (Figure 69). Because the opponent holds his ground, a knee strike becomes a natural completion (Figure 70). As the techniques are performed they simply flow. When completed, it is possible to identify techniques and arts.

Figure 65

Figure 66

Figure 67

Figure 68

Figure 69

However, because a skill looks like a particular art does not necessarily mean that the performer is skilled in a particular art. Many masters have suggested that at a certain level all arts look similar. Skill at a particular range or distance is more important than skill in a particular art. Many JKD concepts practitioners tend to identify kali, muay Thai, silat, and boxing as important arts to know. However, without an understanding of their limitations—range, instructor preference, and individual ability—being able to quote techniques for each art is of little value in self-defense.

Figure 70

This sequence illustrates the principle of arm destruction. Often attributed to kali, arm destruction techniques are found in boxing as well. Against the reverse punch (Figure 71) the author strikes the biceps (Figure 72).

Figure 71

Figure 72

Then follows with an elbow destruct (Figures 73-74).

Figure 73

Figure 74

In a natural flow, the elbow is used to strike the throat (Figure 75). It is again important to note that the opponent's angle of attack, energy, and determination must be evaluated immediately when presenting a counter. Having enough skills to draw from is an outstanding virtue of JKD concepts.

Figure 75

has the best fighting system or theory. The fact is that we all share techniques. Some of us have not yet discovered them or have chosen not to develop them to a skillful degree. What often occurs is that our ethnocentric beliefs inhibit us from realizing the fact that we can use any technique we choose.

All arts may be separated into physical skills and social structure. The term social structure refers to the chain of command, the philosophy of the art, special theories or mannerisms, and the general belief that members who accept the philosophy are part of the art. Everyone who practices ITF tae kwon do, for example, shows Korean values, recognizes General Choi as the philosophical leader and, in general, acts and performs in a certain manner. Individuals who study U.S.A. goju separate themselves from others by the way they perform kata, basics, and sparring. Those who practice JKD (Jun Fan) have typically sought to act in a nonconforming manner; thus, they can be recognized by their preference for street clothes, kali, savate, etc. skills, and a "liberated philosophy."

In Figures 76-80, the author redirects the opponent's jab and follows with a choke and takedown.

Figure 76

Figure 77

Figure 78

Each group tends to provide various degrees of expressed ethnocentrism. Ethnocentrism may be useful for building group identity, but in the martial arts it is often used to limit the potential of the artist. However, certain limitations may be useful. It is a most difficult task for a "liberated artist" to develop the discipline, character, and perseverance found at even the beginning ranks of a proper classical school.

Figure 79

Figure 80

The Value of Tradition

It is the opinion of this writer that classical or traditional martial arts are of great value to this country in general and to the martial arts community in particular. It is the traditionalists who have endured the ridicule of the "liberated artists" and continued to grow in strength and number. When all other physical skills are diminished or defeated, strength in character may alone result in victory.

Although our American melting-pot philosophy has resulted in a positive development of physical attributes and strategies, we have not, as a whole, improved on the Oriental social structure. We have often developed our bodies but not our minds. We must do both.

In this silat-like counter, the opponent is manipulated so that he is completely off-balanced (Figures 81 and 82) and directed toward the ground (Figures 83 and 84).

Figure 81

Figure 82

Presently, there are two schools of thought. There are those who see building character through military methods as being the major reason for martial arts. And there are those who view physical success in self-defense as being the central theme in the practice of martial arts. On the surface, these two views are in conflict. In a typical scenario we are asked to envision the liberated artist cleaning house with the typical traditionalist. Having the freedom to mix physical skills has its virtues in physical

Figure 83

Figure 84

performance. Yet we seldom hear about how the liberated artist recovers from a life-threatening illness, excels in school, or stops to help an elderly person cross the street. These character traits have been largely attributed to the traditionalist.

Combining Two Schools of Thought

Jeet kune do is a most valuable theory for developing martial arts. Unfortunately, some would agree, we have only recently begun to understand the value of its concepts. For years JKD was buried beneath enticing but confusing riddles that sang its praise as an art without boundaries. Ignorance is often a source for ethnocentric remarks. And if ethnocentrism exists in any art, it most assuredly has been prosperous in the promotion of JKD. As we find out more about JKD, it becomes less separated and even more functional.

In previous writings we have defined JKD in three categories: as a social art including members of the JKD family; as a physical art combining the Bruce Lee-influenced Jun Fan arts with the post-Lee-influenced arts of kali and Thai boxing; and as a theoretical offering composed of six interrelated and interdependent principles, including multicultural arts, range or fighting distance, five ways of attack, environment, individual and instructor preference, and "absorb what is useful."

Inside Karate's eminent editor, John Steven Soet, himself an acquaintance of the late Bruce Lee, has rightfully referred to this author's definition as "redactive JKD." In this reference, "redactive" is used to suggest that we have offered a revised definition of the previously undefined concept. The importance of JKD is considerable. No theory of combat has equaled the functional system first devised by Lee. Given the combat efficiency attained when JKD methods are applied, many practitioners have chosen to learn only the combative qualities of what have previously been considered traditional arts. However, redactive JKD theory can be functional for any art without destroying the social structure inherent in the realistic performance of the art.

The six principles of redactive JKD are not in opposition to traditional teaching. As long as we operate from the premise that the physical skills in even the most traditional art have always varied from teacher to teacher, there should be no outstanding reason to reinforce or vary selected skills. The problem occurs when instructors make drastic changes in physical performances, like deleting all kata from a system or dropping a noticeable number of techniques in a haphazard manner.

One may offer the theory that the overwhelming interest in Lee following his untimely death in 1973 resulted in far too many unqualified martial artists using his popular "liberation from the classical mess" theme as justification for the irresponsible alteration

Although karate and judo are seldom employed as arts for JKD concepts, in Figures 85-89 the author demonstrates that the concepts are not limited by style. Against the punch Beasley employs a karate-style double movement that lends itself to an unsecured attack. Realizing that the opponent's energy has moved him forward, Beasley simply lowers his center of gravity (Figure 86) and prepares for a hari-goshi (Figures 87-89).

Figure 85

Figure 86

Figure 87

Figure 88

of many time-honored traditional practices. These alterations, over a period of time, have depreciated the value of karate. Those who promote this theory like to point to current tournament karate as an example of nonrestrained performance in which the plan is to score a point with what looks like a technique that a karate practitioner may have used. Already it appears that traditional skills are being accepted in favor

Figure 89

of the "liberated mess" that may well have led to the fall of tournament karate.

Again it should be mentioned that the traditions—the bow, chain of command, uniform, etc. (known as the social structure)—should be maintained. Building character takes time and perseverance. Hours of drills can be employed to forge a determined spirit. Previous arguments against traditional training have maintained that these rote drills and subsequent mechanical movements are of restricted use in the spontaneous realities of combat. Agreed. At least at the beginning and intermediate levels, the skills do lack the realism in combat application. However, the concept of the drill may be maintained as we vary the skills to reflect the intent of redactive JKD theory.

Grass Roots

It is important to remember that JKD is not bound by any style. One does not have to perform kali to understand JKD.

However, when JKD theory is applied to traditional kali, the performance would, without question, mirror the material taught by Dan Inosanto. It is worth noting that Inosanto continues to embrace the social structures of many arts while incorporating JKD theory.

If one were to apply JKD theory to wing chun and boxing, the end result would undoubtedly resemble the performed skills of Lee and his students, James Lee, Ted Wong, and Jerry Poteet. If one were to apply JKD theory to the concept of grappling, the resulting interpretation may well be the same as that taught by Larry Hartsell. In each case the instructors mentioned are able to teach and perform in a variety of categories.

How, then, can redactive JKD theory (bear in mind that while the theory is independent of all styles, social and physical JKD are reflective of the JKD family, or "clan") be applied to traditional karate and tae kwon do?

Without the theory of social structure, the application of redactive JKD to karate would perhaps be disastrous. Economy of motion is not a prerequisite to many karate and tae kwon do skills. The idea, then, becomes to maintain as much as possible the traditional skills and then supplement them with others. More than anything else, redactive JKD, when placed in a matrix, can be used to identify both our strengths and our weaknesses.

Historically, every master of every style of karate and tae kwon do incorporated skills from other cultures.

The skills of karate have been altered and mixed, swapped and deleted, tried and failed, until the systems that were developed reflected the intent of the founders. Another founder would have gone through the same process of trial and error until he developed a system that best exemplified his individual preference. When a master found a system that best suited his physical and mental abilities, an attempt was made to pass on this dated material to others. Each system was ideally suited for a particular social, political, and structural environment.

While today we may have little need to develop the skills needed to knock a horseman from his saddle or punch through

Feigning was an important concept in original JKD training. In Figures 90-94, the author demonstrates how a low-kick fake (Figure 90) sets up a boxing-style one-two combination (91 and 92) to be followed by a sweep takedown (93 and 94).

Figure 90

Figure 91

Figure 92

Figure 93

Figure 94

bamboo chest protectors—skills that in another time and place were of utmost concern—we still have need of the spirit that assisted the early karateka in meeting life and death with dignity and honor.

Physical vs. Cultural

Some would say that we cannot separate the physical skills from the social skills, that applying the six principles of redactive JKD to traditional karate would be an impossible task. We must disagree. Governed by the same necessity that every founder of every combat style faced, that of matching the skills to the demands of the environment, we can adapt our own karate skills to our own environments. However, we must be careful to avoid the limitations enforced through ethnocentrism.

Redactive JKD theory can be used to help guide this conversion. Karate is an attitude. Karate is a desire for victory in place of potential defeat. If we look at karate and see only the physical, we have indeed found only the pointed finger as we have missed all

In Figures 95-99, Beasley initiates a karate-style initial move but senses the opponent's body weight has shifted (Figure 95). Beasley redirects the punch away from any potential targets (Figure 96), which in turn sets up a takedown (Figures 97-99).

Figure 95

Figure 96

JKD concepts assist the performer in adapting to range, environment, and the opponent's chosen art.

Figure 97

Figure 98

Figure 99

that heavenly glory that was envisioned by the late Bruce Lee.

To a limited degree, each of the six principles of redactive JKD can be found in every karate, kung-fu, and tae kwon do system. Let us take the adjusted view that when Lee heralded the virtues of freeing oneself from the limitations of fixed styles, he intended for his audience to understand that an emphasis must be placed on physical limitations, not social structure. Since, in reality, he made no public mention of any intended separation, many of us sought liberation by foregoing the bow, the respect for one's teacher, the wearing of identifiable uniforms, and other trappings of Oriental etiquette. I believe this was a mistake. Karate is, again, a state of mind (a disposition). One can actualize no limitations in physical freedom and still embrace the values of the traditional dojo.

Locating one's position between the ethnocentric extremes of the classical mess on the one hand and the liberated mess on the other may be a task undertaken for the future benefit of all.

Projections for Future Efforts

While jeet kune do may well be the world's most popular martial art in print, it is in fact not widely practiced. By 1991 I began to reflect on reasons for the lack of interest in actual physical practice. JKD, especially conceptual JKD, has much to offer any art.

The United States has provided an open laboratory for martial arts development. Americans have enjoyed the opportunity to practice firsthand classical and contemporary arts from many nations.

The 1980s provided many lessons for the martial arts. Full-

Of the various arts available, the author prefers a kickboxing method which utilizes trapping and grappling. Identifying personal preference is essential to a complete understanding of redactive JKD concepts. The raised knee in Figure 100 can serve as a fake and a bridge to set up arm immobilization (Figure 101) and destruction (Figure 102), which allow the low kick easy access to the target (Figure 103).

Figure 100

Figure 101

Figure 102

Figure 103

contact karate was heralded as the kick of the decade as promoters tried to capitalize on the "karate" name value for what turned out to be the amateur sport of kickboxing. Another art that experienced a silent death was ninjutsu. The rage among pseudo martial artists in the mid-1980s, it seemed, was that every other guy who couldn't make it in a real martial arts school ended up with three months of karate lessons and a master's diploma in ninjutsu. The public had almost as much interest in these ninety-day ninja as it did in the kung-fu wonders of the previous decade.

With the "sloppy kickboxers" boring us on TV (there were, however, a few great matches) and the ninja assassins ruining our reputations in the media, it was a miracle that the traditional karate, tae kwon do, and kung-fu arts survived at all. A contributor to that miracle was the megablockbuster martial arts movie *The Karate Kid* (parts I, II, and III). For the first time in ages the public was treated to the original values of the martial arts. The concepts of peace through violence—in other words, "walk softly and carry a big stick—" were the major reason that Americans bought into the martial arts in the first place. Now, thirty years later, that feeling of the Oriental mystique, the sense of controlled power and disciplined rage, was being visually portrayed in the cinema.

Toward the end of the decade, the dojos, at least those that survived the ninja wars, could count on a steady flow of new clients. The students of the '90s have already distinguished themselves as being more knowledgeable. After all, they have felt the disorganized despair of the sport karate tournaments, endured the boredom of the kickboxing matches, escaped the ninja's deadly sales

Once again employing arm destruction (Figure 104), this type found in togakure-ryu ninjutsu, the author strikes a pressure point in the arm (Figure 105). He follows with a right hook to the shoulder (Figure 106), completely immobilizing the opponent's weapon before moving in for a left hook (Figure 107) and a leg-destruct counter (Figure 108). The Filipino artists often use the expression that if you destroy the fangs, you destroy the serpent. Boxing hands are fast and powerful, increasing one's potential for quality limb destruction.

Figure 104

Figure 105

Figure 106

Figure 107

Figure 108

pitch, and still managed to find ways into reputable schools.

Students of the '90s want to feel that sense of belonging that can only be found in the traditional school atmosphere. They want to find discipline in an otherwise undisciplined world. The '90s have the potential to begin a new generation (thirty years). Fathers who first took lessons in the '50s and '60s now have sons and daughters with the same kinds of needs that brought them to the dojos several decades ago. The major attraction for martial arts has been and continues to be self-defense. But the student of the '90s doesn't want the realities of the kickboxing match, nor the stealth tactics of the ninja.

Self-defense has certainly been a major theme of the '80s. When the ninja claimed to mix the old weapons with the new, they attracted thousands of enthusiasts ready to see if they did indeed have the ultimate system for self-defense. Predictably, the thousands quickly dwindled into a few hundred divided practitioners as the "secrets" of a once-dead art were revealed.

There are those who argue that JKD is the epitome of the mix-and-match school. In the '80s the late Bruce Lee and his art of JKD

Employing limb destruction again, the author reinforces the effect of the elbow with a hook to the knee (Figures 109 and 110). By quickly moving in, he easily applies a dev-astating left hook (Figures 111 and 112).

Figure 109

Figure 110

Figure 111

Figure 112

once again became the most talked about subject in the martial arts. In spite of the publicity afforded the art, one would be hard-pressed to find a JKD school with more than a dozen students. The point that we are making is that students are interested in learning about, but minimally willing to experience firsthand, realistic combative training.

Arts that have been claimed to be more effective for self-defense (i.e., JKD, ninjutsu) generally attract more students. Arts that have the reputation of being effective for self-defense and can identify with a current known figure (stereotype) who is or has been successful in self-defense also have the potential to attract students. An appreciation for this general rule can be evidenced by thumbing through the martial arts section of any major city telephone directory and noting the numbers of masters, champions, and victors of combat all in search of a limited market. This process continues to be confusing to students who are taken in by claims of grandeur and misleading advertisements.

What we've learned from the kickboxers is that learning to recover from a strike is often just as important as learning to deliver a strike. Self-defense is, in most cases, considered only after the first blow has been thrown. The JKD practitioners have managed to get across the point that one may be expected to react to combat in an environment unlike that of a typical dojo, against an opponent whose attack varies greatly from the prearranged attack of a dojo mate, and at a range that has not been sufficiently covered through standard instruction. In America, it can be said that we have learned and applied much from JKD theory.

Limb destruction is often overlooked in other arts, but it is common knowledge for Filipino arts. In Figures 113 and 114 the author demonstrates leg destruction using the knee.

Figure 113

Figure 114

CHAPTER 4
Basic Training

Bruce Lee and world champion Joe Lewis shared an appreciation for basic training. Lewis was known to finish his workout sessions dripping with sweat. Lee, according to friends, was obsessed with working out. Lee took great pains to build just the right equipment. His two-hundred-pound heavy bag, running shoes, and various wing chun dummies have been examined, tried out, and written about by numerous individuals.

A jeet kune do enthusiast who has carried the tradition of basic training to perhaps a new level is Cliff Lenderman. Known as the "Strongman of JKD," Lenderman possesses a Mr. America-level physique—the result of countless hours of basic training. A former student of master instructors Dan Inosanto, Stephen K. Hayes, Master Chai, and others, Lenderman, true to the JKD premise "absorb what is useful," has developed his JKD concepts methods to a level of perfection. Yet it is his superior physique, demonstrated power, and charismatic personality that set him above the crowd in JKD circles.

Like Lee and Lewis, JKD's "Strongman" spends hours in the gym. Lenderman's focus is on the grappling and striking interpretations of JKD; thus, the need for power and speed becomes evident. Lenderman's workouts incorporate weight training, calisthenics, dynamic tension, aerobics, and skill repetition.

WEIGHT TRAINING

For far too many years weight training has been considered taboo for the martial artist. Muscles, it was believed, impeded speed. The old masters didn't use weights; therefore, it followed that modern practitioners should avoid weights as well. This type of antiquated thinking has continued to retard the development of martial arts. To be sure, too many "masters" get out of shape because they exercise only their minds, not their bodies. It is interesting to note that one of the reasons for the development of what we now call kung-fu fighting was the need to emphasize fitness for the priests of the Shaolin (circa 625 B.C.).

Cliff Lenderman uses a variety of progressive resistance routines. In the following sequence, he demonstrates key exercises designed to increase punching and striking power by building strength in the arms, shoulders, and chest. It is important to focus on specific muscle groups. Lenderman prefers the dumbbells for freedom of movement.

In Figures 115-132, Lenderman performs a variety of exercises for building strength to increase striking power. Included are biceps curls, standing and bent arm laterals, and presses.

Figure 115

Figure 116

Figure 117

Figure 118

Figure 119

Figure 120

Figure 121

Figure 122

Figure 123

Figure 124

Figure 125

Figure 126 **Figure 127**

Figure 128 **Figure 129**

Figure 130

Figure 131

Figure 132

SIT-UPS/PUSHUPS

In performing sit-ups, it's best to elevate the legs for added stress to the exercise.

In Figures 133-137, Lenderman performs sit-ups with legs elevated.

Figure 133

Figure 134

Figure 135

Figure 136

Figure 137

Pushup positions may be varied for added resistance to the chest and shoulders.

In Figures 138-143, Lenderman performs pushups from a variety of positions.

Figure 138

Figure 139

Figure 140

Figure 141

Figure 142

Figure 143

DYNAMIC TENSION

In the absence of weights, a method known as dynamic tension provides a functional substitute. It is important to maintain a variety of exercise routines for basic training. Cliff Lenderman's workout includes free weights as well as machines and a significant amount of aerobic exercise, e.g., running.

In Figures 144-151, Lenderman demonstrates the dynamic tension exercises used for stretching and flexing muscles.

Figure 144   **Figure 145**

Figure 146

Figure 147

Figure 148

Figure 149

Figure 150   **Figure 151**

AEROBICS AND SKILL REPETITION

Shadow boxing: A shadow boxing routine includes aerobic and skill performance routines.

In Figures 152-155, Lenderman demonstrates a few techniques used in his Thai boxing workout.

Figure 152

Figure 153

Figure 154

Figure 155

In Figures 156-185, Lenderman demonstrates focus-pad training.

Figure 156

Figure 157

Figure 158

Figure 159

Figure 160

Figure 161

Figure 162

Figure 163

Figure 164

Figure 165

Figure 166

Figure 167

Figure 168

Figure 169

Figure 170

Figure 171

Figure 172

Figure 173

Figure 174

Figure 175

Figure 176

Figure 177

Figure 178

Figure 179

Figure 180

Figure 181

Figure 182

Figure 183

Figure 184

Figure 185

Focus-pad training: Perhaps the most often used training aid for JKD practitioners is the focus pad. Fighters use the pads to simulate attack and defense methods and to improve skill and accuracy. Single direct attacks such as the front kick (Figures 156-157) and the round kick (Figures 158-159) provide a basic kicking drill.

Hand skills, including the jab (Figure 161), cross (Figure 162), and hook (Figure 163), can be combined with the elbow (Figures 164-165). Defensive skills of parrying and blocking may be practiced by having the coach simulate a jab (Figure 166) or holding technique (Figures 169-170). Combination drills, including elbow attacks (Figures 171-174) and knee-alternate drills (Figures 175-185), are standard practice in Thai drills used in JKD concepts training. The practitioners should work in two- or three-minute rounds with one-minute rest periods. Ten rounds or more are considered basic maintenance training.

Simulated attack/defense drills: Less effective than focus-pad drills, the simulated attack/defense drills are used to perfect focus and timing.

To maintain a high level of fitness and performance, JKD practitioners must practice daily. More often than not, the fight is won by the one who is in the best shape. Once the expert level is attained, continued maintenance exercise will insure skill. However, additional time is required for skill improvement. A typical basic-training routine might include weight training and focus-pad drills for one hour on Mondays, Wednesdays, and Fridays. Tuesday, Thursday, and Saturday routines might consist of shadow boxing and contact sparring. Many experts include running or other aerobic exercise on a daily basis. As the reader can see, JKD-level performance requires considerable basic training.

Figure 186

In Figures 186-203, Lenderman demonstrates elbow (Figures 186-188), parry (Figures 189-190), knee (Figures 191-192), and kicking (Figures 193-198) drills. Combinations including knee and elbow attack (Figures 199-203) can be used to enhance the training routine.

Figure 187

Figure 188

Figure 189

Figure 190

Figure 191

Figure 192

Figure 193

Figure 194

Figure 195

Figure 196

Figure 197

Figure 198

Figure 199

Figure 200

Figure 201

Figure 202

Figure 203

Conclusions and Observations

THE SEARCH FOR THE ORIGINAL STYLE OF JKD

During his lifetime Bruce Lee was fond of repeating a Zen saying that he had adapted as follows: "As far as other styles or schools are concerned . . . take no thought of who is right or wrong, or who is better than."

The development of jeet kune do is not unlike the flowering branches of a spring landscape. There currently exists about a half-dozen interpretations of the art of JKD, each with a valid foundation. As junfanologists we can find merit in all of these interpretations as we objectively weigh the strengths and weaknesses of each system.

Lee's progression through four clearly discernable teaching programs has given rise to a number of fighting methods, each laying claim to a valid interpretation of the art. The Seattle groups often have strong emphasis on the Chinese way of wing chun, as do the Jun Fan groups in Oakland and a portion of the Los Angeles/Chinatown. When Lee was alive, JKD was very much a Chinese form of scientific streetfighting. Joe Lewis has noted that while he was taken with Lee's theories of combat he had no interest in Lee's kung fu. Lewis maintains that Lee was able to bridge the gap, trap, and strike with incredible speed. Lee's strength at 135 pounds was equally impressive. But the techniques that he employed were noticeably Chinese.

The Tao of Jeet Kune Do, Lee's major research effort, emphasizes the importance of speed, power, and sensitivity, the three elements that are most important to Lee's original system. But if Lee's method was so organized, why the change to a fourth teaching style—that of JKD concepts? We know that Lee was most influenced by his Chinese system of wing chun. Yet, after suffering an apparently humiliating if not eye-opening fight with a fellow martial artist, he chose to change his system.

Thus, JKD—the way of the intercepting fist—was conceived as a form of fencing without a foil. Lee's combination of strength, speed, and sensitivity gained through years of wing chun chi sao with his newly created empty-hand fencing method spelled defeat for any conceivable opponent.

During the late '60s and early '70s Lee's concepts of non-chambering, independent motion, ways of attack, and economy of motion were revolutionary when compared to the mechanical forms of the karate-oriented arts. It was conceivable that Lee could train others in his method. Lee's skill has never been disputed. But could he transform others into his image? Maybe, and maybe not.

Perhaps Lee looked about and decided not to share his one-of-a-kind fighting art. Perhaps he did attempt to teach others what he alone had developed. Yet without his speed, sensitivity, and power, JKD, the invincible art, became something less in the hands of others. Of what use is a Porsche to a man who has no gasoline? It is conceivable that Lee recognized the futility of teaching others who lacked his overwhelming dedication to fighting arts a method that they could not, without the same attributes, perform.

So maybe, just maybe, Lee chose to focus on the concepts of his creation. The ways of attack, the concept of flowing from one style to another in response to the dictates of range and environment—these could be taught. They have been taught by Dan Inosanto. Replacing the Chinese heritage of JKD with a Filipino heritage of kali, Inosanto has traveled the world teaching the concepts of JKD through his own family art. It is not surprising that a majority of JKD devotees today view JKD not as a Chinese martial art but as a Filipino art with interest in Thai and Indonesian systems. If, on the other hand, you adopt the philosophy that Lee's JKD developed naturally from wing chun to original art to concepts, you probably would not object to "JKD Society" methods. Indeed it would be considered a natural progression of change.

Creating the Tomb

While few would argue the "concepts" approach as anything less than useful, it is not the system of fighting that Bruce Lee taught to his students. The "concepts" approach has done much for the popularity of Thai boxing and now silat. It is probably the most significant foundation for the current popularity of kali. In fact, one martial arts (kali) newsletter claimed that Lee may have developed JKD after studying kali. What during the preceding decade seemed like a novel way for a few individuals to teach selected arts and still identify with the Lee mystique has now developed into a virtual chain of "concepts" schools, each teaching a curriculum of kali, Thai, and silat and claiming to be JKD-certified.

Of course, this select group of concepts instructors was able to enjoy an enviable income from the perpetuation of these schools. The quest for the gold (income) became so obvious by the late 1980s that some found it necessary to boycott anyone not in the so-called "clan." And while brotherhood and family were always brought out as "the reason why we do it," more than a few nonfamily members were aware of the constant politics and bickering for position and profit.

In spite of the political perils associated with speaking out, a few still asked the question, "What is jeet kune do?" Sure, hitting people with sticks was amusing, striking Thai pads was invigorating, and learning to "flow" from lock to lock could certainly hold your attention long enough to fatten someone's bank account. But what does all this have to do with Bruce Lee? After all, Lee didn't want any schools. He didn't even want any students.

At one time he did teach. People want to know what he taught. JKD enthusiasts really don't want to know how to fish. They want to know how Bruce Lee caught fish. In other words, instead of investigating art after art—which is an excellent method devised by a high level of genius— JKD enthusiasts want to know what Lee performed as an art. How did Lee throw his round kick? Okay, everyone can't expect to perform it like Lee, but how did he throw it anyway? How did he punch? How did he move? What were the seven variations of foot sweeps and the five ways of attack?

JKD is about Bruce Lee. It's not just about concepts and arts and politics and money. If it were, there would be no more questions, and everyone would be satisfied. JKD is people wanting to do what Lee did and think about what Lee thought about. By using the terms jeet kune do, some people have enjoyed fame and fortune and, in exchange, given what they thought was important—most in an honest manner, some with deception at heart. Was the student, the JKD enthusiast, ever consulted? Probably not. If he or she had been, there would have been a very different JKD out there today.

Liberate Yourself from JKD!

What Bruce Lee accomplished through his teaching of jeet kune do has been met with mixed opinions. Some say he ruined traditional martial arts. Others claim that he advanced the arts through his own dedication to study. Magazine editors continue to claim that having Lee on the cover sells magazines. Yet in the established martial arts community—the karate and tae kwon do groups—Lee is seldom mentioned. Lee invariably appeals to the nonfighter—the guy who studies about fighting but doesn't care much for really mixing it up.

An observation made more often than not about JKD seminars is that they tend to attract a large number of nonfighter types who enjoy learning a variety of complex moves, not realizing that their potential for deployment is slight. Yet this dichotomy of thought exists even among tentative observers. Lee taught fighting but he didn't fight. He did work out so hard that even the best fighters agreed he would have been a worthy opponent. The one great fighter in the JKD group, Joe Lewis, remained out of contact with the group after Lee's death.

The fact remains, however, that in spite of the endless politics, the fast-buck artists, and those who use only a chance meeting with Bruce Lee as their claim to fame, Lee has had more effect on the positive development of martial arts than any other man.

Ultimately, his message to us was to use JKD and then toss it aside. Those who use the knowledge but forego the name are the true disciples of Lee. Yet the name JKD has such attraction for so many that they tend to forsake all rational thought simply for the identity. As I write this, the popular phrase is "Bruce Lee's jeet kune do"—as if to make doubly sure the reader understands that they are to be identified with the sifu himself.

It is true that this book is about the fighting method called JKD. For the astute reader there is also the knowledge that the scientific method has been successfully employed in what may well be the most misunderstood art ever presented. JKD for Lee was simple, direct, and uncomplicated. JKD was devoid of gross movements of this style and that.

Both Bruce Lee and Joe Lewis were fond of the forward side hook punch. The two jeet kune do practitioners spent hours viewing films of Marciano, Ali, and other boxers (sometimes using mirrors to reverse the fighting stances). In this sequence Lewis demonstrates the slip (Figures 204 and 205) and follows with a double hook combination (Figures 206-208). Note that the forward leg is used to immobilize the opponent.

Figure 204

Figure 205

Figure 206

Figure 207

Figure 208

Change-ups were a common practice in the original JKD training routines. Here, Lewis demonstrates a fake backfist (Figure 209), followed with a leg destruction (Figure 210) and a forefist strike (Figure 211). Although these skills are commonly practiced in most modern karate schools, it was advanced information during the '60s and '70s.

Figure 209

Figure 210

Figure 211

Figure 212

The practice of interrupting or immobilizing the forward fist (Figure 212) provides a perfect entry for the snapping hook (Figure 213).

Figure 213

In this sequence Lewis demonstrates a form of the intercepting fist by checking the strike (Figure 214) and at the same time striking with the forefist (Figure 215).

Figure 214

Figure 215

Training drills for original JKD students focused on mobility (as opposed to the fixed stances of early karate/tae kwon do schools). Here, Lewis and Jerry Beasley demonstrate give-and-take drills using the side kick (Figures 216-219).

Figure 216

As Lewis recalls, the drills were performed at high speed for several minutes.

Figure 217

Figure 218

Figure 219

JKD is often more easily understood in terms of variation from traditional karate/tae kwon do/kung fu. In Figure 220, Lewis demonstrates the JKD stance. Note that the arms are raised for protection while the legs are positioned for mobility.

Figure 220

Lee was best suited for speed and power. I have been told by Lewis that Lee's gift was his incredible and perhaps blinding movement off the firing line. His initial movement was explosive and nontelegraphing. In short, he could make the intercepting fist work. Those who trained with Lee worked out at such a high level that, against other styles used and taught in the late '60s and early '70s, they,

In Figure 221, Beasley and Lewis square off in the typical JKD posture with arms raised and bodies positioned for defense.

Figure 221

too, moved with such direct and uncomplicated skill that their being defeated was highly unlikely.

By way of comparison, we should note that in 1970 Lewis demonstrated such skill in the kickboxing ring that he was unstoppable. No opponent could last even a few rounds. Lewis retired from competition only to attempt a comeback in the early 1980s. He was defeated in a bid for a national title. At age 39, his skin was easily cut, which resulted in a TKO even though most experts agreed he had won the fight. And while Lewis possessed the skills of a master, it became evident that the competition had been greatly advanced. Independent motion, mobility, economy of motion—concepts virtually unknown in 1970—were common knowledge in 1980 (thanks largely to Lewis, who has been credited with teaching America's best fighters). When both sides know the same strategy, the guy who possesses the superior attributes wins. In this case, age became an attribute.

Lee had both the superior strategy and the superior attributes. Eventually, however, the attributes would have been diminished. Even Lee would find age a worthy foe. JKD, the lightning-fast explosive movement, does not fully work unless the attributes are at a significantly high level. Realizing this, Dan Inosanto promoted the concepts, the strategy, in a manner that could be used in all arts, not just Lee's chosen method of modified wing chun/kickboxing.

Through the promotion of the concepts, JKD could forever be superior. JKD as a concepts method does not match one person's attributes against another's. JKD concepts promote strategy—which arts, which range, and under which environmental conditions that combat exists. My art becomes your art in that I understand your strategy. If your art is about trapping, I understand trapping. If your art is about kicking, then I, too, understand kicking. "The once fluid man crammed and distorted by the classical mess" has restricted his strategy to promote only the virtues of his system. The classical man fails to recognize his own limitations.

JKD concepts are about recognizing, experiencing, and avoiding limitations. The strategy of JKD concepts values the ability to absorb useful information from any art. JKD concepts view arts not in terms of historical or cultural arts, but in terms of the arts' functions at kicking, punching, trapping, and grappling ranges. What I can learn about fighting in various environments from a particular art is a typical JKD concept.

JKD concepts can be seen as a cannibal art. In effect, it seeks to absorb only the functional skills, leaving the essence of the art—its kata, cultural trends, and beliefs—for the classical man. The application of JKD concepts can result in a superior strategy or a pathetic "jack of all trades" who has collected so much information that he is eventually betrayed by his own limitations. The principle of chiseling away the nonessentials is often misapplied by the concepts advocate. To chisel away nonessentials of an art might be virtuous, but at what point do we stop chiseling away at different arts? When is enough enough?

To experience JKD I feel that one must have an understanding of both the original art and the concepts method. The two interpretations are very different. To have anything less is to be trapped in a particular time and place.

What Bruce Lee taught and performed in 1968 is very different from what he promoted in 1973. The concepts method that Inosanto has advanced during the 1980s is at still a different level than what Lee had achieved. If JKD is truly a never-ending experience, then how can one claim to teach it? What Lee tried to teach others about JKD can be applied today.

An article I wrote for *Karate International* that had found even a wider audience by 1992 examined the attraction of the name JKD and how the name has become more important than the practice.

HAS JKD BECOME THE REAL MUTANT TURTLE?

We know that Bruce Lee intended JKD to be intensely physical. He was fanatical about working out. Let's suppose that, at some point, Lee reviewed his students' JKD skills and realized that without the physical development that he personally enjoyed, they could never make the techniques work. Perhaps he had discovered a self-defense method that worked, possibly better than any other.

Not unlike the seven-foot-tall basketball player who scores repeatedly with a slam dunk, Lee could show others what he could do. Without his physical ability, however, they could not duplicate his skill.

So, let's speculate, Lee concluded that without the physical level achieved only after years of devotion, his students could not really perform JKD—at least not at Lee's level. He could teach them the technique, but that alone does not insure success. Well, you can't go to your students/disciples and say, "Look guys, this JKD stuff just isn't working out the way I thought. It's just not happening." So JKD was destined to become a philosophy. You can beat up the students, and you can win with superior technique—JKD or not. But you can't defeat philosophy. You can debate it, but you can't make it disappear.

What Lee was doing in 1970 was unique—in 1970. But by

1990, much of the JKD information—nonchambering, economy of motion, independent motion—was common knowledge.

Realizing that skill and technique will always be improved (witness the history of any sport), Lee no doubt would have moved to the concepts method. Concepts, like philosophies, are independent of the people who claim to express them. Now I don't think that, had Lee survived, the vehicle for JKD would have been kali, Thai, or silat. Nor do I think that the traditional/classical JKD techniques would have gone unchanged.

However, in view of the fact that most JKD fans will only be able to see the technique and not recognize the concept, I would argue that original JKD offers a more tangible method for recreating Bruce Lee's JKD, which is what most people want. Yet the concepts—not to be confused with specific arts, as is typically the case—comprise a higher order of intellectual inquiry and probably would have been the avenue pursued by Lee.

In the final analysis, the "real JKD" is gone. We know that Lee moved JKD from one level to another, from what is now called original JKD to the concepts method. What we don't know is whether there could have been a third level. Had Lee survived, would not this third level have been the "real JKD"?

All this talk about clan, family, lineage, style, and rank pertains to the "boat." If, as Lee suggested, we are to discard the boat once we have crossed the water, what does this say about those of us who teach and perform (or even write about) JKD? And what of those who just want to be on the "boat," with no destination in mind? Have they collectively lost the meaning of JKD? Is experiencing the boat more valuable than where it can take us, or have we become mutant turtles carrying our boats (shells) as part of our identities?

JKD is discarding the boat. It also means being free of clever disguises like Jun Fan or Bruce Lee's art. JKD has been killed by commercialism. Everything Lee imagined in the 1971 *Black Belt* article "Liberate Yourself from the Classical Mess" has become reality. He wrote: "What originated as one man's intuition . . . was transformed into . . . fixed knowledge . . . a holy shrine but also a tomb in which they buried the founder's wisdom." The wisdom of Lee continues to be buried in competition, politics, jealousy, and ignorance.

Today, JKD has come full circle. What we now call JKD *is* the classical mess. JKD is now replete with authorities who profess to own knowledge of JKD (and will sell this knowledge for anything from a few thousand bucks for a seminar to a few Hamiltons for a correspondence course). One man's intuition has certainly become, in Lee's own prophetic words, "solidified, fixed knowledge, complete with organized, classical responses presented in logical order" (*Black Belt*, September 1971). The end result, as Lee envisioned, has been "divisive with vigorous condemnation and a lot of self-justification."

Yet amidst all this rubble is some valuable information. But to ride the boat you must first possess a ticket. Only the most dedicated junfanologist could hope to extract knowledge and not be stayed by the political B.S. (become a prisoner on the boat). The next time you hear someone claim to be an instructor of jeet kune do, Jun Fan, etc., ask why he continues to be burdened by a useless boat or shell. Is he truly a giver of the truth, or has he betrayed his identity like so many others for the glory of the mutant turtle?

TO POSSESS THE TICKET

JKD is very much an advanced philosophy. JKD is an expression against fixed styles. As such it is best experienced by the individual who can identify with the fixed style. The best JKD practitioners have been those who first earned black belts in traditional styles. And perhaps this is the ticket.

Both Dan Inosanto and Joe Lewis, the two great proponents of JKD, utilized JKD to perfect their own arts, kali and karate, respectively. Lee became an expert in wing chun before he developed JKD. Inosanto once called JKD "problem solving." I can think of no better way to describe it. All arts have limitations. JKD is the science of recognizing and solving problem areas within an art.

Those practitioners who express their JKD as a little of this and a little of that are probably on the wrong course. Lee was an expert in a particular method, not simply a performer of various methods. Apply the redactive JKD matrix to your own style or method. At a lecture in North Carolina, I worked with a number of JKD practitioners to help solve the problem limitation areas in their individual systems. The matrix provides a concrete example of strengths and weaknesses. Where you are strong, advance. Where you are weak, seek instruction. Experience arts that fit your own interests and abilities. Above all, practice, train, spar, research, and discover.

Remember, JKD is not simply a matter of joining this organization or that, of studying this art or with that instructor. JKD is the freedom to react, the knowledge to respond, and the ability to discover. If you possess those qualities, you need no one's approval or recognition. You are JKD. Your thirst for knowledge will invariably lead you to many paths and help introduce you to many teachers. Each experience will be unique. And now, as Lee was fond of saying, "Walk on . . ."

Your journey begins today.

About the Author

Dr. Jerry Beasley is considered to be America's foremost martial arts educator. A university professor (Radford University, Radford, Virginia) with a doctorate in education, Beasley earned his seventh dan in 1991 from former world champion and mentor Joe Lewis. As a consultant since 1980, Beasley has worked with more than eight hundred martial arts school administrators worldwide in the areas of curriculum design and management training. As an author, he has published three books and more than eighty articles. And in the field of promotion, Beasley has developed the Karate College summer camp to a premier event. Researching, writing, promoting, and consulting are for Beasley simply ways of teaching and developing the martial arts.

His research on JKD has advanced the art from myth and riddle to principles of scientific inquiry.